Faith and Politics
in a World Gone Awry

Faith and Politics
in a World Gone Awry

By
STEPHEN W. PLUNKETT

WIPF & STOCK · Eugene, Oregon

Wipf & Stock
An Imprint of Wipf and Stock Publishers
199 W. 8th Ave., Suite 3
Eugene, OR 97401

www.wipfandstock.com

PAPERBACK ISBN: 978-1-5326-3746-9
HARDCOVER ISBN: 978-1-5326-3747-6
EBOOK ISBN: 978-1-5326-3748-3

Manufactured in the U.S.A.   01/11/19

This book is dedicated to our two children, Stephen and Alison, with deep gratitude for their lives, and for their faith in Jesus Christ.

Contents

Acknowledgements

I extend my heartfelt thanks to my wife, Margaret Currie Plunkett, for her unfailing support throughout the process of writing this book. Not only did she read the entire manuscript before I sent it to Wipf & Stock and offer her critique and skill as an excellent proofreader, but she put up with me during my writing, which was no small feat.

I also extend my deep thanks to my sister-in-law, Alison Currie Meier, who has taught several languages both in the United States and in Germany, and who is a superb grammarian. She was willing to come in at the very end of this project, and read the entire manuscript over a single weekend from a grammatical standpoint. I know that the final product is better because of her work and I am grateful to her for being willing to share her skill.

My deep thanks are extended to my two brothers-in-law, James S. Currie and Thomas W. Currie III, for the time they spent reading the manuscript and for their critique of it in advance of publication. I also give my gratitude to a dear friend, Nancy J. Duff, the Stephen Colwell Associate Professor of Christian Ethics at Princeton Theological Seminary. We have been friends since we were students together at Austin College in Sherman, Texas, more years ago than I care to count. She also read my manuscript in advance of publication and offered her forthright and honest critique, and I thank her from the bottom of my heart. James's, Tom's, and Nancy's critiques all made the book better than it would have been had I been left to my own devices and desires. Whatever shortcomings are in the book belong to me.

Introduction

A llow me to begin by saying that I deeply love the church and am thoroughly committed to it. My hope is that whatever challenge you might hear in this book is rooted in that love and commitment. I believe that what really matters in life is Jesus Christ—his birth into this world as Emmanuel, God with us, his life lived in complete faithfulness to God, his death on the cross on Good Friday, and his resurrection on Easter morning. This defines reality for me and is the reason I have written this book.

One could, I suppose, read what I have written as though it suggested that getting the world out of the mess in which we find ourselves is all up to us. I hope you won't hear that, because that is *not* what I intend. There is, however, a certain discipline involved in being a disciple of Jesus Christ, and what I hope you will hear in the coming pages is an emphasis on that discipline, which results in a deep commitment to the Christ of the cross and empty tomb, for our hope is in *him*. He has borne in his body on the cross all of our sins and failures and risen victorious on Easter morning over them, as well as over all the other signs of human self-destruction. And the Holy Spirit brings this good news to life in the lives of those who are committed to the crucified and risen Lord *for the sake of all creation.*

I also begin with the basic assumption that the pure, free, un-adulterated, grace of God stands at the center of the gospel of Jesus Christ, and therefore, of the Christian faith. I'm not talking about grace as a concept, but grace as it is lavishly given in the person of

Jesus Christ. This is grace that cannot be earned and that certainly no one merits, yet it is given simply because God loves the world that God has made and the entire human race. I understand that everything I have to say in this book grows out of the grace of God that we experience in Jesus Christ. Some of the things I have to say, in my mind, are quite challenging, that is, the polar opposite of the way many Americans sometimes think. It will be important to remember what I have said at the beginning about grace. My understanding is that I'm talking about the Holy Spirit bringing the grace of God to life in the flesh and blood of our lives.

Let me illustrate this with a parable of Jesus, a parable that makes a bold and daring claim about the sheer generosity of the grace of God. In Matthew 20:1–16, Jesus tells a parable about a landowner who goes out in the early morning to find laborers who are willing to spend the day working in his vineyard. He goes to the marketplace where day laborers congregate and finds some willing workers, all of whom agree to work for the usual daily wage for a laborer. At nine o'clock, the landowner finds others standing idle in the marketplace, and because there is plenty of work to be done, he hires them as well, promising that, at the end of the day, he will pay them what is right and fair. The landowner returns to the marketplace about noon and again at three o'clock, each time finding more workers for his vineyard. Finally, he goes back to the marketplace one hour before quitting time only to find people still standing around and complaining that no one has hired them. So he says to them, "You also go into my vineyard and get to work."

At the end of the workday, the landowner calls together all the workers and pays them their wages. Payment is not made in a private, sealed envelope, but is open for all to see. No doubt to everyone's surprise, the five o'clock workers get paid first, and lo and behold, they receive a full day's pay. You can just imagine what the all-day workers are thinking and how their eyeballs practically turn into dollar signs. Much to their dismay, however, they are paid exactly the same amount—a full day's wage to which they had agreed when they were hired. They are incredulous, and they make no secret of the fact that they are outraged by the sheer injustice of it. After all, they have worked all day in the hot, blazing sun. Surely they deserve more pay than those who worked only part of the day! They grouse and complain, a matter that comes to the attention of the landowner, who says, "'I am doing you no wrong; did you not agree with me for the usual daily wage? Take what belongs to you and go; I choose to give to this last the same as I give to you. Am I not allowed to do what I choose with what belongs to me? Or are you envious because I am generous? So the last will be first, and the first will be last'" (Matt 20:13b–16).

The core issue comes to the fore at the end of the parable where the landowner asks the piercing question, "Or are you envious because I am generous?" The underlying problem of the all-day workers is their fury with the utter generosity of grace. We read this parable, of course, as a word about God, and it paints a picture of how generously God gives away divine grace. Perhaps like the all-day workers, we want the grace of God to be a matter of deserving, and we want to think that we deserve it because we've done a reasonably good job with our lives. After all, isn't a relationship with God something a person can earn or merit? We crave the notion that we are not equal to others; we are better. But the gospel of Jesus Christ has a huge problem with this orientation toward God, and as the parable so aptly says, we should never assume that the way we live determines God's disposition toward us. God's disposition toward us grows out of *who God is*. The God of the gospel is the God *who loves us with the love that will never let us go*, and this is why the incarnation of God in Jesus Christ is "good news of great joy for all the people" (Luke 2:10b). And it is the reason that grace stands at the center of the Christian life.

I also want to share with you at the outset some basic assumptions that I bring to the table about faith and politics in a world gone awry. These assumptions lay a basic framework for the discussion I propose to have:

1. Being a disciple of Jesus Christ is the basic commitment on which all other loyalties and allegiances are based.

2. The values inherent in the gospel of Jesus Christ take precedence over all other claims of loyalty, even loyalty to the United States of America. Sometimes the values of one are diametrically opposed to the values of the other. Part of being a disciple of Jesus is being able to tell the difference and having the courage to "speak the truth in love" (Eph 4:15a).

3. Following Jesus takes precedence over being a Democrat or a Republican, a so-called "conservative" or "progressive."

4. The gospel of Jesus Christ does not merely augment the way we view God, neighbor, self, and world, but is the primary source of the way we view God, neighbor, self, and world.

5. It is not the Christian's job to force a Christian worldview on everyone else in society, but it is the Christian's job to live from the perspective of a worldview that is true to the gospel and to participate in the body politic in ways that are faithful to the God who has claimed, loved, and redeemed us through the sacrifice of the cross.

A Re-Description of Reality

William H. Willimon notes that George Lindbeck said that when preachers teach and preach scripture, they engage in a complex re-description of reality.[1] I find this to be constantly true of the gospel. Take Luke 4:16–30 as a prime example. Jesus, visiting his hometown synagogue in Nazareth on the Sabbath Day, was asked to stand and read from scripture and was handed the scroll of the prophet Isaiah. The custom was that scripture not only be read, but also commented upon. So Jesus reads parts of Isaiah 61 and 58 in which God's anointed one brings good news to the poor, proclaims release to the captives, the recovery of sight to the blind, and lets the oppressed go free. It is a message of exuberant liberation, of freedom, of joy, and of tearing down the dividing wall of hostility that separates people. And yet as excellent as this good news

---

1. Willimon, *Preaching Master Class*, 89.

sounds, there's a problem lurking in the background to which we shall come momentarily.

Every eye in the synagogue is fixed on Jesus as the congregation gives him its rapt attention. When the reading is complete, Jesus says, "Today this scripture has been fulfilled in your hearing." They are all amazed at the gracious words that come from Jesus' mouth. Can't you just hear them exclaiming, "Aren't we proud of him, our hometown boy! We just knew he'd grow up to be a preacher!"

The scene, however, is about to take a nasty turn because this congregation has a view of God's love for people that is different from the view found in their own scripture. He in essence says, "Despite all of your praise, 'no prophet is accepted in the prophet's hometown,'" (Luke 4:24) that is, *if the prophet tells truth*. And with that, Jesus enters forbidden territory. "[T]he truth," says Jesus, "is there were many widows in Israel in the time of Elijah . . . [when] there was a severe famine over all the land" (Luke 4:25). Yet Elijah was sent to none of those widows in Israel. Instead, Elijah was sent to a widow at Zarephath in Sidon. A huge problem, though, was that the widow at Zarephath was a Gentile, and Elijah was sent to this outsider rather than to a fellow Israelite. Moreover, while he was there, the Gentile woman's son died, and through the power of God, Elijah called him back to life. Now can you see how the blood began to boil in that hometown crowd?

But that's not the end of the story. Jesus continued by saying that "[t]here were also many lepers in Israel in the time of the prophet Elisha, and none of them was cleansed except Naaman the Syrian," which means that God chose to heal a Gentile leper instead of an Israelite leper! And at this everyone in synagogue was filled with rage. The text doesn't say that the crowd got angry or a little upset or disgruntled. It uses the strong language of *rage*. They got up right then and there, drove their hometown boy out of town, led him to the brow of a hill from which they intended to hurl him off. They were going to kill him on the spot and be done with this troublemaker, but Jesus went on his way, having passed through the midst of them.

Can't you just hear the congregation? "This isn't what we believe! This isn't what we came to the synagogue to hear. This message is entirely too political and doesn't belong in the synagogue. The preacher has gone to meddling in our personal values, beliefs, and attitudes toward others. If we'd sat there long enough, he'd be telling us that the love of God is unconditional and universal!"

That, of course, is exactly what the text says: *God's love is unconditional and universal.* Jesus was offering a re-description of reality, and it was one that his hometown congregation could not stomach.[2] Before we point our finger at them, let us be honest about ourselves. Like that first century congregation, the idea that God's love is unconditional and universal is what many people in today's political milieu simply cannot stomach, even people who are in a pew every Sunday.

This book is about politics in which people learn to love those who are radically different from themselves, even Muslims in a nation where Muslims are regarded by many as a threat to our national well-being and security because many Americans believe that Muslims are all radical Islamist terrorists, which could not be further from the truth. But I'm also speaking of refugees who come to the United States, seeking asylum and longing for protection from the threat of personal violence in their home country. One of the main themes of the Gospel of Luke and indeed the gospel itself is that, in Jesus Christ, God is tearing down every wall that divides human beings, tearing down all the hate and bigotry that stands between people. This is the re-description of reality that needs to take place in our nation's politics today.

Addressing Politics through the Lens of Faith

This book is written from the conviction that faith in Jesus Christ shapes the whole of the Christian life, not just the parts that are safe and convenient, requiring little if anything of us. The realm of

2. Christians should be careful not to use this passage to criticize the Jewish community. Since we are reading the text as Christians, we need to apply it to ourselves.

faith involves not only the interior life of the spirit, but everything that disciples of Jesus Christ think and do and are, including the way we participate in the politics of our communities, nation, and world.

The online *Merriam-Webster Dictionary* says that the word "politics," among other definitions, means "the opinions that someone has about what should be done by governments: a person's political thoughts and opinions," and I am posing the question, "What shapes those thoughts and opinions?" Each of us holds a personal worldview that forms the way we participate in public life in general, and the way we vote in particular. It is often the picture in our heads that is decisive—the way we envision God, neighbor, self, and world. This book is an effort to examine these foundational concerns by dealing with the *theological* framework within which political choices are made. My experience as a pastor for thirty-eight years is that theology often goes straight out the window when it comes to politics. The Bible, people often think, is about one's spiritual life but one's politics belong in a different sphere, being about life in the real world where tough decisions need to be made based on one's sociopolitical perspective. But what does the gospel say to people who want to make sense of today's political landscape not first and foremost as Democrats or Republicans, conservatives or progressives, or even true-blue patriotic Americans, *but as disciples of Jesus Christ*? Said another way: What would it mean if the claims of the gospel were to shape the way we think and behave in the body politic?

While I am reluctant to begin a book with a disclaimer, let me say what I do *not* mean when I say that our faith should both inform and shape our politics. I do *not* mean that we are to put blinders on and view every political issue through a very narrow lens that those on the evangelical "right" say is Christian. Neither do I advocate an approach to politics that presumes that we can carry the essential tenets of the gospel around on a convenient list in our pocket on which to rely when hard-hitting political choices need to be made in these perilous times. On the other hand, I do not advocate an approach that suggests that a purely left-wing ideology is in order. The stakes are much too high for either of these approaches.

I've heard it said, "When I go into the voting booth, I vote for what's best for my family and me." But what if one's frame of reference were infinitely larger than "my family and me"? What if we were to understand that, when we go into the voting booth, the gospel calls us to cast our vote based on convictions rooted in our faith? As a pastor, I have often observed a monumental disconnect between one's personal discipleship and the views that Christians espouse about public issues. In fact, it seems to me that many church members are more concerned with being true to their Democratic or Republican ideology than with God's perspective on the glaring issues that threaten the very survival of the planet on which we live.

The Bible is filled with images of God's purpose for creation, and time and again, the biblical writers make the claim that human life is rooted in the intention and will of God. There is no paltry evidence in the Bible of the just and loving society God would have us build, and this is the substance of the gospel with which we need to be vigorously wrestling within the faith community. For example, what role does the gospel play in shaping our views of God, neighbor, self, and world? What does it mean that the community of the baptized is the glad harbinger of the politics of God's realm in today's world? And what, after all, *are* the politics of God's realm? Does anyone know? Are there at least provisional answers to this question? If so, where do we get our clues?

In my experience, church members have typically shied away from such potentially volatile discussion, saying that a discussion of politics doesn't belong in the church. One of my presuppositions, however, is that the church is a community that should be able to have this difficult discussion even amid disagreement, because of our overriding unity in the Christ who empowers us to "speak the truth in love" (Eph 4:15a) to each other. I am envisioning a community of faith that actively wrestles with the politics of our nation and world in light of the narrative of scripture, a community that does so "with all humility and gentleness, with patience, bearing with one another in love, making every effort to maintain the unity of the Spirit in the bond of peace" (Eph 4:2–3). In the words of Dietrich Bonhoeffer:

> God has willed that we should seek and find God's living Word in the testimony of other Christians, in the mouths of human beings. Therefore, Christians need other Christians who speak God's Word to them. They need them again and again when they become uncertain or disheartened, because living by their own resources, they cannot help themselves without cheating themselves out of the truth. They need other Christians as bearers and proclaimers of the divine word of salvation."[3]

Are we not called to this kind of humility, mutual forbearance, and communal spirit? A key purpose of this book is to encourage such discussion within the church, inspired by the words of a familiar hymn, "Blest be the tie that binds our hearts in Christian love: The fellowship of kindred minds is like to that above."[4] When hearts are bound together in Christian love, it is possible to enter into the most difficult discussion of the thorniest subjects. We need not fear one another in this discussion, for as members of Christ's church, we are at the basic core of our beings brothers and sisters in Christ.

Facing the Reality of Our Context

Sometimes when Christians interpret the Bible they do so as what I call purists. That is, they want to insist that the text involved has an original meaning that is not to be confused by the contemporary context in which we live. But I believe it is impossible to have either a worldview or an interpretation of scripture that isn't shaped in large measure by the context in which we live. The discussion the church has been having with the LGBTQ[5] community is a case

---

3. Bonhoeffer, *Life Together*, 32.

4. John Fawcett, "Blest Be the Tie That Binds" (1782).

5. LGBTQ: Lesbian, Gay, Bisexual, Transgender, Queer.

in point. The denomination in which I serve has a document entitled The Confession of 1967, which says:

> The Bible is to be interpreted in the light of its witness to
> God's work of reconciliation in Christ. The Scriptures,
> given under the guidance of the Holy Spirit, are nevertheless words of human beings, conditioned by the language, thought forms, and literary fashions of the places
> and times at which they were written. They reflect views
> of life, history, and the cosmos which were then current.
> The church, therefore, has an obligation to approach the
> Scriptures with literary and historical understanding. As
> God has spoken the divine word in diverse cultural situations, the church is confident that God will continue to
> speak through the Scriptures in a changing world and in
> every form of human culture.[6]

One's context shapes in a foundational manner the way that one reads and interprets the Bible, not to mention the way one interprets national and world events. For example, many churches are interpreting God's work of reconciliation in Christ *in our context* by embracing gay men and women as brothers and sisters in Christ and approving same-sex marriages. They do so by a willingness to hear God's word anew in the context in which we are living, opening ourselves to what we know today about sexuality from the perspective of such disciplines as biology, sociology, and psychology that were totally unknown to the biblical writers. Similarly, the Parable of the Great Judgment (Matt 25:31–46) will be heard differently by a homeless person who finds dinner in a dumpster than by a middle- or upper-middle-class American who wines and dines in style. A Third World Christian living in the shackles of hardship and poverty will have a nuanced reading of the story of the exodus that may be all but unintelligible to someone living in the affluence that so many of us take for granted. For the starving populations in various parts of the world, the Parable of Lazarus and the Rich Man (Luke 16:19–31) is the anguished cry of the world's poor to dismantle societal structures that grind the poor

6. *The Confession of 1967—Inclusive Language Version*, 9.29.

into the dust of the earth, but for a middle- or upper middle-class citizen of a First World country, it may be heard as a modest call for a few more dollars of easy charity.

Given the fact that our context is such a powerful ingredient in how we hear and act upon scripture, it is essential that, as we open God's word, we also open our hearts and minds to the plight of others who live in radically different contexts, realizing that a large part of our calling is

> to unmask idolatries in Church and culture,
>
> to hear the voices of peoples long silenced,
>
> and to work with others for justice, freedom, and peace.[7]

To insist on seeing the world only from one's own point of view is to commit a grievous sin against the rest of humanity. A large part of learning to love the neighbor as the self is learning to walk, however feebly it may be, in the neighbor's shoes.

Allow me to say this before going any further. We are all sinners. None of us is perfect and it is impossible for any of us to live in total faithfulness to Jesus Christ. As Philip Yancy has pointed out:

> How easily we forget that the church was founded by disciples who betrayed their master. None was willing to stand by Jesus as the religious and political authorities condemned him to death. At his moment of greatest need, the disciples fled in the darkness. The boldest of the lot, Peter, was the very one who cursed and denied him three times before the cock crew. It was for traitors that Jesus died.[8]

My emphasis is on the good news that *the grace of God given in Jesus Christ* is at the center of this book. Following him, we come to understand who God is and how we are called to live, however provisionally and imperfectly that may be.

---

7. "Brief Statement of Faith," lines 69–71.

8. Yancy, *Soul Survivor*, 285.

The Contour of This Book

What I have just suggested, however, is not an easy road to travel. It goes without saying that there is no single reading of scripture, and that committed Christians interpret the Bible in diverse and often contentious ways. My point simply is that *this is the discussion we need to be having in the church,* and as we have this discussion, as Paul says it, we are to "clothe ourselves with compassion, kindness, humility, meekness, and patience," and above all "with love, which binds everything together in perfect harmony" (Col 3:12, 14). Furthermore, I propose that congregations submit themselves to the corporate discipline of viewing these perilous times through the lens of faith, and that congregants learn to help each other along this difficult journey.

In the hope of offering some grist for the mill, the contour of this book begins with a discussion of what it means to reach out in love to the neighbor who is radically different, and to do so as children of the Old Testament character of Abraham by whom God promised "all the families of the earth shall be blessed." Next there is a chapter that addresses the basic building blocks that help to establish a theological framework for the choices we make, looking specifically at what it means to see God, neighbor, self, and world through the lens of faith in a way that fosters God's new creation in Jesus Christ. After that, I turn to a frank discussion of the exodus and the cross and resurrection, and how redemption itself is a *political* act. We then consider the politics of taking care of God's good creation, taking care of each other as brothers and sisters in the same family, and overcoming the temptation to keep the gospel small and manageable. Then there is a chapter on politics as social justice. And finally, there is a chapter on the fear of the "other" that we all face today not just as Americans but in the global community as well.

In no way do I suggest that I have mastered any of these topics. This simply is a provisional look at some basic building blocks given to us by the gospel as we attempt to live our political lives in faithfulness to Jesus Christ.

Questions for Discussion—It is assumed that these questions will lead to a conversation that involves exploring the Bible. Please use scripture in giving your answers to the following:

1. Do you believe that one's personal context plays a significant role in biblical interpretation?

2. When you go into the voting booth, does the gospel of Jesus Christ have a place? Explain your answer.

3. Do you agree that one's politics should be viewed through the lens of the gospel? Why or why not?

4. Do you believe that the grace of God is so central to the Christian life that it should play a role in your politics? Say why or why not. What role does grace play in your life?

1

Learning to Love the Neighbor
Who Is Different

A book like this begs two questions, "Why talk about faith and politics now? And what is there in today's cultural milieu that leads us to do so?" My short answer is that the politics of our day place our nation, as well as the entire global community, in a very vulnerable position. I'm talking about a combination of factors: the vulnerability of people without health insurance, a heightened sense of suspicion about so-called illegal aliens in our midst, and the lack of concern for the well-being of everyone in our own American community, not to mention the entire global community of which we are only one part. Even if the current political climate is short-lived, we and the rest of the world will be dealing with its ramifications for years to come.

So let's begin this chapter where we left off in the discussion of Luke 4 in the Introduction, namely, with the good news that *God's love is unconditional and universal*. While this emerges from the essential nature and character of the gospel itself, we first see it in the call of Abraham in Genesis 12:1–9. There God comes to Abraham and God commands that he "Go from your country . . . to the land that I will show you" (Gen 12:1). But in the wake of the command is an amazing promise that God is going to make of Abraham "a great nation." Now, mind you, this command and promise are to a landless, childless man and his wife Sarah, who are both as old as the hills. And on top of it all, Sarah is barren (Gen 11:30)! Just to be clear: God comes to a childless couple in old age and promises to give them a child. Never mind the fact that Sarah is both barren and way past the years of childbearing and never mind the fact that, a little later in the story, Abraham laughs his head off at God's promise and asks, "Can a child be born to a man who is a hundred years old? Can Sarah, who is ninety years old, bear a child?" (Gen 17:17). In the very next chapter Sarah herself laughs at the idea that she will have pleasure in her old age. Afterwards, God asks Abraham, "Why did Sarah laugh, and say, 'Shall I indeed bear a child, now that I am old?' Is anything too wonderful for the Lord?" (Gen 18:12).

That is the point: Nothing is too wonderful for the Lord, and this is why, in the call of Abraham in Genesis 12, God assures Abraham that from his lineage an entire nation will come and then gives another unmistakable promise: "*in you all the families of the earth shall be blessed*" (Gen 12:3b, emphasis added). God has promised, through Abraham's progeny, to bless all people on earth. The first eleven chapters of Genesis, often referred to as the primordial history or pre-history,[1] ends with the story of the Tower of Babel, and if one did not know the rest of the story, he or she might ponder whether the story will even continue or if the creation God pronounced "very good" in Genesis 1 has been lost forever. But as soon as one begins to ponder this question, it becomes clear that God is far from finished with creation. Through one man, Abraham, and his wife Sarah, God reaches out to reclaim a lost creation. God never gives up on this promise (see Romans 9–11), and we can be sure that one day we shall realize this promise

1. Scholars suggest that in Genesis 1–11 we are not yet dealing with history per se, except in the sense that it records the experience of the entire human race in every age and culture. The story of Adam and Eve, for example (as suggested by the word *adam*, translated "humankind"), is the story of everyone. History enters the picture with the call of Abraham and Sarah in the twelfth chapter with the promise of land and progeny.

in all its fullness. We do not know how or when; the Bible contains no blueprint. In the meantime, however, we are called to live in the light of this promise, recognizing that God loves all people, not just those of whom we approve and with whom we agree, *but all people*, as evidenced by God's lavish promise to Abraham.

The Call of Abraham and Sarah

The call of Abraham and his and Sarah's subsequent "going forth" form an excellent paradigm that grows out of the soil of the universal impulse of biblical faith. Theologian and Professor Miroslav Volf writes this about the *departing* required in the biblical narrative:

> Sarah being barren (Genesis 11:30), the command to "go forth" placed before Abraham a difficult choice: he would either belong to his country, his culture, and his family and remain comfortably inconsequential or, risking everything, he would depart and become great—a blessing to "all the families of the earth." If he is to be a blessing he cannot stay; he must depart, cutting the ties that so profoundly defined him . . . The courage to break his cultural and familial ties and abandon the gods of his ancestors (Joshua 24:2) out of allegiance to a God of all families and all cultures was the original Abrahamic revolution . . .[2]

To say that the gospel is for everybody can be dangerous, especially in today's political climate in the United States where we see an alarming return to nationalism at the expense of the global community. Fearing that the global community is a threat to our national security and way of life, we have heard a great deal about "America First!" Many of the prevailing political voices, even inside the church, shun the idea of being a blessing to all the families of the earth because they want God's blessing to be for America first. Cutting the ties that profoundly define us out of allegiance

2. Volf, *Exclusion and Embrace*, 38–39. In this quotation, Volf makes reference to Brueggemann, *The Land*, 15ff.

to the God of all families and all cultures is like an idea from an alien world, and if you stand up for such beliefs, it can cost you dearly. For example, if a person says that God loves Muslims as much as Christians, he or she can lose friendships. It simply goes against the grain to say that God loves every person on earth indiscriminately and unconditionally. But this is the good news of the gospel. Paul says it this way, "Just as Abraham 'believed God, and it was reckoned to him as righteousness,' so, you see, those who believe are the descendants of Abraham. And the scripture, foreseeing that God would justify the Gentiles by faith, declared the gospel beforehand to Abraham, saying, 'All the Gentiles shall be blessed in you.' For this reason, those who believe are blessed with Abraham who believed" (Gal 3:6-9).

The Gentiles are loved by God and justified by God through faith? Really? Yet this is not only the story of Abraham and Sarah but is also the story of the cross and the empty tomb of Jesus Christ. To the church in Corinth, Paul writes, "For since death came through a human being, the resurrection of the dead has also come through a human being; for as all die in Adam, so all will be made alive in Christ" (1 Cor 15:21-22).

This is a very timely topic that does not play too well in the part of the Bible belt in Texas where I live. For many people, the idea that Jesus Christ died on the cross and rose from the grave *for all people* is an outrageous aberration of the gospel. After all, the gospel is for our kind of people who have "accepted Jesus." Yet the gospel calls us to live for the neighbor, whoever the neighbor may be. Jesus Christ is not anyone's private domain but belongs to all kinds of people who have been given a place at the table in God's realm. In this regard, Volf, offers these words: "[U]ltimate allegiance of those whose father is Abraham can only be to the God of 'all families of the earth,' not to any particular country, culture, or family . . ."[3] In other words, *we are not Americans first and foremost, but disciples of Jesus Christ.* That is who we are at the very core of ourselves.

3. Ibid., 39.

There is a distinct sense in which this all sounds rather outlandish and utterly foolish, that is, if we are using conventional thinking as a standard. To embrace the universal love of God for all creation is to open wide the door to people who are different from us, and that is enough to get a person killed, the death of Jesus by Roman crucifixion being the prime example. The gospel addresses us by saying in more ways that we can fathom, "If your love for me is as deep as you say it is, then it will be as deep and high and wide as all creation." And while it is difficult to swallow on any given day, Volf writes:

> Much like Jews and Muslims, Christians can never be first of all Asians or Americans, Croatians, Russians, or Tutsis, and then Christians. At the very core of Christian identity lies an all-encompassing change of loyalty, from a given culture with its gods to the God of all cultures. A response to a call from that God entails rearrangement of a whole network of allegiances. As the call of Jesus' first disciples illustrates, "the nets" (economy) and "the father" (family) must be left behind (Mark 1:16–20). Departure is part and parcel of Christian identity . . .[4]

The Demands of a Faith That Runs Deep

One of the major problems we face in the church today is the fact that many Christians crave a less scandalous faith. We want a religion that doesn't ask too much of us but gives us everything on our wish list. We hanker after a God that suits us, a religion in which the love of the gospel is all about easy charity—a hand-out here and a hand-out there, a turkey for a needy family at Thanksgiving and a nice juicy ham at Christmas—in other words, the kind of charity that doesn't cost us anything in the long run, and above all, doesn't impinge on our lifestyle. In other words, we prefer a charity that is carefully calculated so that it doesn't keep us from doing the things we really want to do like spend money on ourselves.

4. Ibid., 40.

While the gospel of Jesus Christ insists that we be generous with sharing what we have, it has nothing to do with this kind of cheap, easy charity, or with maintaining a moderate religion. The Lord of the church has no interest in or stomach for it. The call to follow Jesus Christ is a call to full-bodied love for the neighbor, and by the grace of God, we can come to see every person on earth as our neighbor, a neighbor whom we are called to love as a brother, a sister.

One of the most pressing issues, if not *the* most pressing issue before us today, is learning to love the neighbor who is radically different, even those perceived to be enemies. Many Americans believe that Muslims are their enemy, because it is often assumed, as I have said, that all Muslims are radical Islamists. This, of course, breeds all kinds of enmity and hostility on both sides, the result being that we fear each other, and fear leads to the poison of hate, and the poison of hate leads to open conflict. Israelis and Palestinians pit themselves against each other. "Death to America" is the political chant that has been used in Iran since the Iranian Revolution began in 1979, and the entire world knows that Iran and Israel harbor the most vehement hatred for each other. This list of tribal, religious, and national conflicts continues ad nauseam, and the reasons for those conflicts are complex. *The point simply is that we must break the cycle of hatred by learning to understand the adversary, and Christian congregations should be laboratories for understanding in a way that enables us to love the neighbor who is different.* This is both the legacy and the power of the cross. And for anyone who thinks this is alien to our culture, it is for many Americans! Or that it leads to foolishness and weakness, it does! Paul, however, says that "God's foolishness is wiser than human wisdom, and God's weakness is stronger than human strength . . . God chose what is foolish in the world to shame the wise; God chose what is weak in the world to shame the strong" (1 Cor 1:25, 27). Miroslav Volf writes of his personal experience with the question at hand:

> After I finished my lecture Professor Jürgen Molt-
> mann stood up and asked one of his typical questions,

both concrete and penetrating: "But can you embrace a četnik?" It was the winter of 1993. For months now the notorious Serbian fighters called "četnik" had been sowing desolation in my native country, herding people into concentration camps, raping women, burning down churches, and destroying cities. I had just argued that we ought to embrace our enemies as God has embraced us in Christ. Can I embrace a četnik—the ultimate other, so to speak, the evil other? What would justify the embrace? Where would I draw the strength for it? What would it do to my identity as a human being and as a Croat? It took me a while to answer, though I immediately knew what I wanted to say, "No, I cannot—but as a follower of Christ I think I should be able to."

. . . My thought was pulled in two different directions by the blood of the innocent crying out to God and by the blood of God's Lamb offered for the guilty. How does one remain loyal both to the demand of the oppressed for justice and to the gift of forgiveness that the Crucified offered to the perpetrators? . . . I felt that my very faith was at odds with itself, divided between the God who delivers the needy and the God who abandons the Crucified . . .[5]

Many of us are caught between these alternatives in the perilous times in which we are living. What is the meaning of the cross for a faith "at odds with itself"?

I feel the need to dig in a little further at the point. You may disagree with Volf about the ability to embrace the enemy, and if you do, I am in agreement. For example, no one is asked to embrace her abuser—not even a Christian. But if we can't embrace the enemy, we can certainly, in faithfulness to Jesus, love the enemy enough to pray for him or her. Jesus does not tell us to bury our heads in the sand, and a rape victim should not heed the conservative Christian's advice to tell victims of rape to forgive the perpetrator and not report what happened to the police. Jesus says in the Sermon on the Mount, "You have heard that it was said, 'You shall love your neighbor and hate your enemy.' But I say to you,

5. Ibid., 9.

Love your enemies and pray for those who persecute you . . ." (Matt 5:43–44). Even if we cannot embrace the enemy, which many victims of violence cannot do, we certainly can pray for the enemy. Another illustration that comes to mind is ISIS.[6] Certainly, the gospel doesn't demand that we embrace the adherents of ISIS, but Jesus does ask us to love them enough to pray for them, to ask that God be at work in their lives to change their hearts and remove their lust for hatred and killing and other forms of violence, as well as to pray for God's ultimate forgiveness of them.

Unscrambling the Categories and the Centrality of Scripture

American Christians today need to unscramble the categories that we often use to label others and ourselves. If I think of myself as a conservative person, then I run most of the issues through my conservative filter. (I once had someone tell me, "You have to understand that I am extremely conservative, and I'm only interested in conservative points of view.") Likewise, if I am a progressive person, I run the political issues of the day through my progressive filter. The point is that, in both cases, the filter to which I am committed plays a powerful role in where I end up. I understand that, in many cases, this is an oversimplification. There are, after all, many moderate American Christians who espouse neither the politics nor the tactics of the far left or the far right. But what poisons the very atmosphere in which we live is the virulence of conservatives and progressives who are interested in no outcome other than the one to which their preconceived ideological bent leads them. What might happen to the character of political dialogue if we would all seriously entertain the question, "What if the situation is more complicated than I've allowed myself to see, and what if I'm wrong?"

Dietrich Bonhoeffer suggests that regardless of how right we think we are, in the end we could discover that we are wrong. Only

---

6. ISIS: Islamic State of Iraq and Syria.

God has the final word. Paradoxically, this allows us to take a stand for what we believe to be right and just, but always with the caveat that our views are, in the end, always subject to the judgment of God. Here are Bonhoeffer's words: "Christian life is the dawn of the ultimate in me, the life of Jesus Christ in me. But it is also always life in the penultimate waiting for the ultimate."[7] When everyone acknowledges this, then civil conversations and acceptance of others become more possible.

The reality of the subjective is, of course, impossible to escape. We each live in our own context and we bring the particulars of our context to any political discussion. But what if Christian discipleship involves the discipline of trying to see beyond our personal context? What we need is a clearer picture of who Jesus Christ is, because he is the one who matters. In the big scheme of things, what does God want not just for us in our personal context, but *for all humanity*? We see this in Jesus. And what if looking to Jesus were one of the cornerstones of our faith? *That* is what we want, isn't it? Above all, Christians want to be not conservative or progressive, but *faithful disciples of Jesus Christ who embody the divine love revealed in the narrative of scripture and in Christ's life, death, and resurrection.* Some people will be conservative, others will be progressive, and still others will be moderate, but being such is never a matter of first priority for disciples of Jesus. In other words, we are to be rooted in the call of God to offer the world hope when on many days there seems to be little reason for hope; rooted in the vision of the God who makes a way where there is no way; rooted in the willingness to make personal sacrifice for the sake of the common good; rooted in the ethics of loving the neighbor as the self even when it means "loving your enemies and praying for those who persecute you" (Matt 5:44); rooted in the joyful spirit of storing up "for yourselves treasures in heaven, . . . [because] where your treasure is, there your heart will be also" (Matt 5:20–21). The key is embodying the narrative of scripture.

When I speak of being disciples of Jesus who embody the narrative of scripture, I'm talking about personal beliefs, values,

7. Bonhoeffer, *Ethics*, 168.

and yes, politics that *bear the character of Jesus Christ* because, first and foremost, we belong not to any political party or ideology, but to him. In fact, the rest of this book will make little sense apart from this central claim. For disciples of Jesus Christ, the biblical story is the filter through which the issues of the day need to be sifted. The narrative of scripture describes who we are and who we are called to become by the grace of God. This is why Bible study is so much more than simply learning the facts of the story. The goal of Bible exploration is internalizing the story until it becomes so much a part of the fabric of our lives that it actually shapes and forms the people we are becoming. Eugene Peterson has said it this way:

> Christians feed on Scripture. Holy Scripture nurtures the Holy Community as food nurtures the human body. Christians do not simply learn or study or use Scripture; we assimilate it, take it into our lives in such a way that it gets metabolized into acts of love, cups of cold water, missions into all the world . . .[8]

Discussing the transformative power of language, Peterson continues:

> It is the very nature of language to form rather than inform. When language is personal, which it is at its best, it reveals; and revelation is always formative—we don't know more, we become more. Our best users of language, poets and lovers and children and saints, use words to *make*: make intimacies, make character, make beauty, make truth.[9]

Fueled by the Spirit of the risen Lord, the story of scripture *makes* disciples of Jesus Christ who, over a lifetime, "grow up in every way into him who is the head, into Christ" (Eph 4:15b), and learn to live their lives—even their political lives—in response to the unearned and undeserved grace of God.

8. Peterson, "Eat This Book," 6.
9. Ibid., 7.

As I said in the Introduction, the unearned and undeserved grace of God is central to the Christian life, and therefore, is what life in the church is all about. Not rules and regulations or about good people and bad people, but "amazing grace, how sweet the sound, that saved a wretch *like me*."[10] Living the Christian life is mainly about seeing the world through this lens, and the church is called to be a laboratory for doing so as we help one another along life's journey.

Questions for Discussion— It is assumed that these questions will lead to a conversation that involves exploring the Bible. Please use scripture in giving your answers to the following:

1. What do you think Abraham's and Sarah's "going forth" has to do with the lives we lead?

2. Do you agree that the love of Jesus Christ is for everyone? Why or why not?

3. Do you think people in the church today are looking for a less scandalous faith than what God asks of us?

4. What do you personally believe about loving neighbors who are different, such as Muslims?

5. What do you make of Moltmann's question to Volf on pages 19–20? Is he onto something or not?

6. What do you think it means to allow our politics to bear the character of Jesus Christ?

---

10. Newton, "Amazing Grace" (1779), emphasis added.

2

Imagining a New Creation

We want only to show you something we have seen and to tell you something we have heard . . . that here and there in the world and now and then in ourselves is a New Creation.

—PAUL TILLICH, *THE NEW BEING*[1]

People of good will arrive at vastly different conclusions about candidates, political parties, and the issues at stake in any election. So let's put aside, at least for the moment, all the hot political topics about which our nation is sorely divided. Instead, I want to address the basic building blocks that help to establish a theological framework for the choices we make. While I do not presume a single theological framework (mine!), I do hope this is useful in pointing to some of the fundamental questions that help to shape a person's theological mindset or temperament.

---

1. As quoted by Frederick Buechner, *Now and Then*, on the page immediately preceding the Introduction.

Two Parables of Jesus to Consider

God rarely if ever settles for the status quo. The faith of the Bible is not concerned with affirming the world as it is, but with closing the gaping disconnect between the way the world is and the way God calls the world to be in Jesus Christ. A great deal of the Bible is an invitation to envision the world in a new way and one's own life with fresh imagination. The parables of Jesus, for example, inevitably call for a fresh imagining of God, neighbor, self, and world. Consider the Parable of the Lost Sheep in Luke 15:3–7, in which Jesus likens the realm of God to a shepherd who has lost one of his one hundred sheep. The shepherd leaves the ninety-nine behind and goes in tireless search of the single lost sheep, refusing to stop searching until the lone, lost sheep is found and safely back in the fold. When the shepherd finds the lost sheep, he lays it on his shoulders and rejoices, takes it home, and throws a huge party. "Rejoice with me," he exclaims to his neighbors, "for I have found my sheep that was lost" (Luke 15:6b).

Now on the face of it, this parable seems to make an utterly ridiculous point. Who in his or her right mind would leave an entire flock of sheep vulnerable to the hazards of the night just to find one sheep that was dumb enough to get separated from the flock? But that is conventional wisdom speaking, and most of the time the Bible speaks non-conventional wisdom. We glimpse how strikingly non-conventional this parable is when read in the context of Luke 15. In the first two verses, we discover that Jesus tells the Parable of the Lost Sheep in a wave of criticism leveled against him by religious leaders. Jesus has been socializing with lowlifes such as tax collectors and sinners, and "the Pharisees and the scribes were grumbling and saying, 'This fellow welcomes sinners and eats with them.'" Therefore, Jesus concludes the parable with this observation: "I tell you, there will be more joy in heaven over one sinner who repents than over ninety-nine righteous persons who need no repentance" (Luke 15:7). Conventional wisdom said that the likes of tax collectors and sinners were trash and anyone with half a brain knew that. They had no place in God's realm, because God's realm was reserved for the "righteous ones," who fulfilled the letter of the law and believed that God judges a person based on whether she or he has more credits than debits in the Great Scorebook of Life. But Jesus is tinkering with the picture in our heads by introducing an entirely new way of imagining the realm of God, one that has nothing to do with credits and debits, but with the realization that *our only hope is divine grace*. And there we have it—a jarring nudge to envision life in a new way that is stunningly centered in the mercy of a God who is willing to do literally everything necessary to seek and to save the lost. No wonder the poet, Francis Thompson, once wrote a poem entitled "The Hound of Heaven." That's how God is—a Heavenly Hound who refuses ever to give up on us but searches relentlessly until the human race is in the arms of grace.

Or consider the Parable of the Sower in Matthew 13:3–9. A sower goes into the field to sow seed. Some of the seeds fall on the path and are devoured by birds. Other seeds fall on rocky ground. With no depth of soil, they are unable to take root, and the sun scorches them. Other seeds fall among thorns and are choked. But some of the seeds fall on good soil, and the harvest is plentiful—in some cases a hundredfold, in some sixty, and in some thirty.

One of the marvels of this parable once again is the dauntless presentation of non-conventional wisdom. I am no farmer and frankly don't know the first thing about it, but as a total novice, it seems obvious to me that the sower should have been more careful in planting the seed. You would think that a prudent farmer would carefully prepare the land before the first seeds were sown. The weeds would have been uprooted, and the field plowed and prepared in the most meticulous manner. Furthermore, would not the farmer take care to avoid sowing seed on the path where some would be trampled underfoot, and others left for the birds to eat? And surely the sower wouldn't cast seed onto rocky soil or among thorns that would no doubt choke the vulnerable young sprouts. Quite to the contrary, however, the realm of God, says Jesus, is like a farmer who slings the seeds of God's grace indiscriminately.[2] And here is the most amazing part of all: This indiscriminate farmer

---

2. On this point, see Long, *Matthew*, 147, and Boring, "Gospel of Matthew," 303–6.

reaps a harvest that is nothing short of miraculous. Thirtyfold would have been a respectable harvest, but a hundredfold would have been beyond the farmer's wildest imagining. And Jesus, of course, wasn't really talking about a fictitious farmer planting seed in a hypothetical field. He is talking about life in the realm of God. God's grace, says Jesus, is indiscriminate. Referring to the Parable of the Sower as the "watershed of the parables," Robert Farrar Capon speaks of the *catholicity* of the kingdom of God described in this parable. Capon writes, "The idea of the catholicity of the kingdom—the insistence that it is at work everywhere, always, and for all, rather than in some places, at some time, and for some people—is an integral part of Jesus' teaching from start to finish."[3] Our preconceived ideas about "good" people and "bad" people are turned upside down. The grace of God is not just for the "right" people who do and say the "right" things, and, of course, hold all the "right" beliefs and affirm the "right" positions on social and political issues that conform to my own. No, the realm of God concerns the lavish planting of the seeds of divine grace, a planting that is accompanied by the sure and certain conviction that the harvest will be more plentiful than any human dares to imagine. And there, once again, we have it—the brazen encouragement to imagine God, neighbor, self and world in a radically new way.

Is There an Alternative Conception of Reality?

I have used these two parables to illustrate a point I believe is central to scripture, namely, that the gospel boldly imagines that the qualities of God's realm depicted in these parables can actually take shape in the flesh and blood of our lives. This is why the apostle Paul says, "So if anyone is in Christ, there is a new creation: everything old has passed away; see, everything has become new!" (2 Cor 5:17). The words of Paul Tillich at the beginning of this chapter assure us that, while the new creation is not yet fully

---

3. Capon, *Parables of the Kingdom*, 73.

manifest, "here and there in the world and now and then in ourselves is a New Creation."

One of the tough realities in the life of faith is dealing with what I suggest is the gaping disconnect between the way the world is and the way God calls the world to be, because left to our own devices, we become centered on ourselves rather than Jesus Christ. The truth is that the realm of God described in the two parables above is quite alien to the values and mores of our culture. In this regard, we often underplay the power of the imagination of scripture to open us up in fresh ways to the new creation that has already dawned in the life, death, and resurrection of Jesus Christ. Too often, engulfed in our own culture, we fail to wrestle with the imagination to which the Bible invites us over against the conventional wisdom of our culture. Somewhere between the two is ample room to wrestle with the realities of the gospel in our lives and in the world at large. Old Testament scholar Walter Brueggemann offers this quote from *Minding the Law* by Anthony G. Amsterdam and Jerome Bruner:

> All cultures are, inherently, negotiated compromises between the already established and the imaginatively possible . . . Cultures in their very nature are marked for *contests for control over conceptions of reality*. In any culture, there are both canonical versions of *how things really are and should be* and countervailing visions about *what is alternatively possible*. The statutes and conventions and authorities and orthodoxies of a culture are always in a dialectical relationship with contrarian myths, dissenting fictions, and (most important of all) the restless powers of the human imagination. The dialectic between the canonical and the imagined is not only inherent in human culture, but gives culture its dynamism and, in some unfathomable way, its unpredictability—its freedom.[4]

We often blithely accept the "canonical versions of *how things really are and should be*" in lieu of wrestling with "countervailing

---

4. As quoted by Brueggemann, *Introduction to the Old Testament*, on the page after the dedication.

visions about *what is alternatively possible*" through the grace and power of the gospel. For it is precisely in the gospel of Jesus Christ that we see how things truly are in the realm of God.

We live, for example, in a nation that teaches us that our ultimate security in life is a prospering economy, that the best way to live the American dream is as consumers who are affluent enough to buy literally everything we want, and that the best way to protect the American way of life is with bombs and bullets. Thus, a strong economy and a superior military are the key to a promise-filled future.

The gospel, on the other hand, offers the portrait of Jesus being nailed to a cross and raised from the dead on Easter morning, proclaiming that herein *and herein alone* is the key to a promise-filled future. Furthermore, we live in a global culture that pits people against one another based on race, ethnic origin, and religion. Many Americans are suspicious of the Muslim world, believing that all Muslims are like the extremists who espouse the proliferation of terror, which, as I have suggested, is a hugely unfair generalization. In other words, a large part of holding one's own in today's volatile climate is fueled by fear and hatred of the neighbor, especially the neighbor who is different. Therefore, Israelis and Iranians often fear and hate each other, as do Israelis and Palestinians, Indians and Pakistanis, or closer to home, Democrats and Republicans, gays and straights, and the list is endless.

In American culture, the gulf between the rich and poor is ever-increasing, as we experience a dwindling middle class. Millions of Americans have no access to the health care that many of us take for granted. We say that we are a peace-loving society, yet we find ourselves in wars that seem to have no end in sight. Our culture teaches girls that the way to be feminine is by being small enough to wear size zero, and there are plenty of people who buy into that notion. And if boys want to learn how to be real men, the culture says it's all about being macho. Success and happiness are all about one's look, one's façade, so there is plastic surgery costing obscene amounts of money, and Botox in abundance.

Somewhere in the midst of these "canonical versions of *how things really are and should be*," God calls us to ask the hard questions about idolatry and faithfulness, and to engage our imaginations in plumbing the depths of scripture for "countervailing visions about *what is alternatively possible*." As we do so, we come to see that what is truly real is the story of Jesus Christ, and in particular, the vision of Good Friday and Easter. That is what makes the difference, leading us to a fresh, new understanding of what discipleship to Jesus Christ is all about.

Cornelius Plantinga Jr. recalls a scene from the movie *Grand Canyon* in which the car of an immigration attorney stalls in a less than desirable part of town. He phones for a tow truck, "but before it arrives, five young street toughs surround his disabled car and threaten him with considerable bodily harm." The tow truck, however, shows up just in the nick of time and "begins to hook up to the disabled car." When the toughs protest, the truck driver takes the leader of the group aside for a not-so-gentle heart-to-heart: "'Man,' he says, 'the world ain't supposed to work like this. Maybe you don't know that, but this ain't the way it's supposed to be. I'm supposed to be able to do my job without askin' you if I can. And that dude is supposed to be able to wait with his car without you rippin' him off. Everything's supposed to be different than what it is here.'" Plantinga goes on to suggest that "central in the classic Christian understanding of the world is a concept of the way things are supposed to be. They ought to be as designed and intended by God, both in creation and in graceful restoration of creation. They are supposed to include peace that adorns and completes justice, mutual respect, and deliberate and widespread attention to the public good."[5]

Self-Interest vs. the Public Good

Widespread attention to the public good is part of the calling to deny the self, take up one's cross, and follow Jesus. And it will arise

5. Plantinga, *Not the Way It's Supposed to Be*, 7–8.

only as people begin the lifelong journey of reimagining God, neighbor, self, and world in a way that is consistent with God's self-revelation in scripture. Indeed, God rarely settles for the status quo. Yet so many of us are caught up in the status quo to such an extent that we are unable, if not unwilling, to see beyond it—*especially if the status quo is working in our favor*. If the system is working in one's favor, why tinker with it? Why hope for something else? Walter Brueggemann's perspective is deeply convicting:

> "[H]ope does not appear among the managers of the status quo. They may be optimists or progressives or evolutionists or developmentalists, but they are not the most likely to be ones who hope. People excessively committed to present power arrangements and present canons of knowledge tend not to wait expectantly for the newness of God.
>
> In the historical narrative of Israel, we may see this reality among the kings and priests, the managers of the status quo. Regularly these leaders are juxtaposed to the prophets who are the voices of hope in Israel. The prophets intend that priests and kings should listen and be open to the risk of the future, but characteristically they do not do so. Characteristically priests and kings seek to silence prophets and crush the voice of hope because they find this voice too threatening . . . The reaction of those in control to . . . a critical word of hope is to become defensive, to attempt to keep the future from impinging on the present in any serious way . . ."[6]

Is not this same defensiveness, as well as the desire of those who manage the status quo to do everything necessary to protect their turf, a prevalent theme in American politics today? No one who is in control wants to lose it, and no one wants the other "side" to win. But something is going to have to give for the common good to be served rather than one "side" or the other winning. Disciples of Jesus Christ are called to tell a different story with the lives we lead. And "to attempt to keep the future from impinging on the present" goes against the very grain of scripture. To open

6. Brueggemann, *Hope within History*, 84–85.

"the present to the surprise of the future" is part of what it means to live in God's new creation. And in these perilous times, congregations are called to find the courage to become communities that nurture the practice of reimagination by working to reshape the picture in our heads of God, neighbor, self, and world. Such an undertaking is not easy; it indeed takes tremendous courage, requiring that we examine the status quo with deliberate objectivity and brutal honesty.

Andrew Young tells the story of his daughter and how she was raised in the very bosom of the church. He faithfully took her to Sunday school and worship every Sunday morning and, early on, he could tell that the gospel was making a significant impact on her life and for this he was extremely grateful. But one day, she came home and announced that she was leaving because she had heard God's call to join forces with Habitat for Humanity and leave for Uganda where she would help build houses for the poor. This was shortly after the fall of Idi Amin, and Uganda was a violent place—both volatile and dangerous.

Andrew Young tried to talk his daughter out of going. Yes, he wanted the gospel to be at the center of her life and for Jesus Christ to claim her for his purposes in the world. But surely that could happen somewhere other than Uganda! What he really wanted for his daughter was that she marry a nice young man, settle down, and raise a family. Anything but Uganda! But God had claimed her life with "countervailing visions about *what is alternatively possible*," and to Uganda she went.[7] May I suggest that Andrew Young's daughter was modeling what it means to reimagine God, neighbor, self, and world?

In his book *Lest Innocent Blood Be Shed*, Philip Hallie tells the powerful story of André and Magda Trocmé and their courageous response during World War II to the demands of the Nazis. André was a pastor in the small French village of Le Chambon, and he and his wife led the effort to shelter over five thousand Jewish children in and around their village, saving them from certain death in the gas chambers. When the government learned of their activities,

---

7. Copenhaver, "It Can Be Dangerous," 9.

they demanded that the Trocmés disclose the whereabouts of all the Jews they were hiding. When they refused, André was thrown in jail.

Why does a person choose to act not out of self-interest, but out of of interest in the welfare of the neighbor? And why does she or he do so when the consequences will undoubtedly result in imprisonment? May I suggest that André Trocmé refused to disclose the whereabouts of the Jews they were hiding because his imagination was shaped by the Bible to which he was committed, the scripture that didn't just inform him, but *formed him*? He had glimpsed a new creation, a creation where "[t]he wolf shall live with the lamb, the leopard shall lie down with the kid, the calf and the lion and the fatling together, and a little child shall lead them" (Isa 11:6). In other words, he was imagining a new world because he had discovered through faith in God that "here and there in the world and now and then in ourselves is a New Creation." Because he knew that the new creation has already dawned in Jesus Christ, he was willing to pursue "countervailing visions about *what is alternatively possible.*"

As it turned out, when the arresting officers arrived at the parsonage to take André to jail, it was suppertime, and Magda invited them to sit down at the table and eat with them before they took her husband away. Hallie writes:

> Later, friends would say to her, "How could you bring yourself to sit down to eat with these men who were there to take your husband away, perhaps to his death? How could you be so forgiving, so decent to them?" To such questions she always gave the same answer: "What are you talking about? It was dinnertime; they were standing in my way; we were all hungry. The food was ready. What do you mean by such foolish words as 'forgiving' and 'decent?'"[8]

What is it that enables people to act with kindness toward someone who intends to do them harm? How is such uncommon kindness even possible? It grows out of glimpsing the new creation of God

8. Hallie, *Lest Innocent Blood Be Shed*, 18–20.

in Jesus Christ. Again, it has to do with reshaping the picture in our heads of God, neighbor, self, and world. And this means that the grace of God can really come to life inside us.

Even if one's high school years were long ago, we can all remember what it was like to feel trapped in a smothering network of cliques. One day, a tenth-grade girl decided to disentangle herself from that network by choosing to befriend a girl outside her immediate circle of friends. Her immediate circle told her in no uncertain terms that she could either be friends with them or with the outsider, but not both. She told them that she wanted to be friends with everyone, and she was willing to suffer the consequences. Somewhere along the way, this young girl had discovered "countervailing visions about *what is alternatively possible.*"

This discovery, however, is not one that typically makes the world go around. In our culture, personal sacrifice is rarely seen as a favorable option. "What's in it for me?" is more to the point. Creation is damaged almost beyond repair, justice for the poor and homeless is trampled upon, demonizing those with whom one disagrees is commonplace (just listen to today's political rhetoric), and attention to the public good is displaced by naked individualism and personal greed. But the good news of the gospel is that this is not the way it has to be. For "here and there in the world and now and then in ourselves is a New Creation." In Christ, we have been set free from the shackles of self-interest. In forgiving our sin, God has opened up a new way of life. And, in this new life, Jesus calls us to explore "countervailing visions about *what is alternatively possible.*" My point simply is this: The political landscape of our nation desperately needs this kind of exploration.

Questions for Discussion—It is assumed that these questions will lead to a conversation that involves exploring the Bible. Please use scripture in giving your answers to the following:

1. In this chapter Robert Farrar Capon is quoted as saying, "The idea of the catholicity of the kingdom—the insistence that it is at work everywhere, always, and for all, rather than in some places, at some time, and for some people—is an integral part

of Jesus' teaching from start to finish." Do you agree with that statement? Why or why not?

2. Why do you think it is so difficult for people in the church to explore "countervailing visions about *what is alternatively possible*"? Why do you think we are so locked in to the status quo?

3. Do you agree with Walter Brueggemann's statement that "people excessively committed to present power arrangements and present canons of knowledge tend not to wait expectantly for the newness of God"? Why or why not?

4. What do you think it means to reimagine God, neighbor, self, and world? Is it a lifelong process? To what extent do you believe it involves an in-depth exploration of the Bible?

3

Redemption as a Political Act

The exodus of Hebrew slaves from Egypt marks the beginning of salvation history in the Bible. One of the most remarkable aspects of this is that it is a *peculiarly political act* in which God personally turns upside down the political realities in the empire of a Pharaoh in ancient Egypt. A band of Hebrew slaves that had lived in servitude to Pharaoh for over four hundred years is set free by the merciful God who hears and responds to the cries of oppressed slaves, and takes sides against the empire, against the protectors of the status quo. Imagine the political impact! No wonder Pharaoh didn't want the slaves to leave Egypt for a new-found freedom! It would destroy Egypt's economic order! Walter Brueggemann speaks of "the capacity of God to transform power relations and bring to well-being those who are 'low and despised' and without claims of priority."[1] Furthermore, says Brueggemann, "The powerful grace of God is a scandal. It upsets the way we would organize life."[2] This, in large measure, is what the exodus is all about. In freeing the slaves, God upends a power arrangement that profits the powerful on the backs of the downtrodden. Let us turn now to the story itself.

1. Brueggemann, *Genesis*, 208.
2. Ibid., 216–17.

Exodus: Compassion, Redemption, and Freedom

Many centuries before the exodus, God promised to Abraham and Sarah both abundant land and progeny (Gen 12:1–9). Abraham and Sarah, advanced in years, received a mind-blowing promise of awe and wonder. The land toward which God was leading them would be a rich land, one flowing with milk and honey. And the descendants of Abraham and Sarah would be "as numerous as the stars of heaven and as the sand that is on the seashore" (Gen 22:17). It would end up being, however, a long and circuitous journey to the fulfillment of God's promise for there would be no instant gratification in this story. In the intervening years, after it seemed to Abraham and Sarah that God had long forgotten the promise that their progeny would be numerous, a son named Isaac was finally born (Gen 21:1–7). Isaac had two sons, Jacob and Esau (see Gen 25:19–34; 27:1–40 for the scheming and conniving of the younger Jacob, aided by their mother Rebekah, against the elder brother Esau). And the twelve tribes of Israel would one day be named for Jacob's twelve sons. Of all his sons, however, the youngest one, Joseph, was Jacob's favorite—a fact that Jacob made no attempt to hide and Joseph was abundantly fond of flaunting in the presence of his older brothers. This favoritism was so blatant that Joseph was the object of his brothers' all-out hatred. In fact, they despised Joseph so much that, in an effort to rid themselves of him forever, they first conspired to kill Joseph, then decided to dump him in a pit, until finally reaching a definitive conclusion about what to do with Daddy's pet. They arrived at that conclusion when a cadre of traders came by as they were eating their lunch. They would sell Joseph into slavery in Egypt (see Gen 37–50 for the Joseph saga).

While Joseph was in Egypt, he rose to prominence in Pharaoh's court through his ability to interpret the dreams of Pharaoh. In fact, by the time Joseph was reunited with his brothers and father some years later when they came to Egypt to escape a famine, Joseph was Pharaoh's second in command. Now one would expect Joseph, in the intervening years, to have harbored a deep hatred for his brothers because of what they had done to him. After all, their betrayal had been brutal. One of the most amazing parts of the story, however, is that Joseph did not, upon his reunion with his brothers, seek revenge against them. Instead, he greeted them with totally unexpected grace, as their scheming cruelty was lavishly forgiven. In fact, Joseph even went so far as *to implicate God* in his brothers' dastardly treachery. Joseph said to his brothers, "Even though you intended to do harm to me, God intended it for good, in order to preserve a numerous people, as he is doing today" (Gen 50:20). Joseph's words and actions go entirely against human instinct, don't they? We typically want people who are guilty of unspeakable cruelty to get their just deserts. To be sure, the Bible certainly speaks of justice and punishment of wrongdoers as we will see in the story of the Israelites fleeing Egypt, but it does so alongside stories portraying the abundance of God's grace. Consider the Parable of the Prodigal Son, for example. And in this story of Joseph and his brothers, consider that in God's new creation, the once scheming brat of a brother has grown to show his brothers *and us* a picture of God's new creation alive and well in human life.

In due course, however, Joseph, his brothers, and their entire generation died, and we read that "the Israelites . . . multiplied and grew exceedingly strong, so that the land was filled with them" (Exod 1:7). This was at a time when a new Pharaoh arose over Egypt, who did not know Joseph, and saw the numerous Israelite people as a potential threat of the highest order to national security. He determined that, because the Hebrew people were more numerous than were the Egyptians, they should be dealt with shrewdly, so that they would not, in the event of war, be able to join the anti-Egyptian side. So the plot thickened, and Pharaoh set taskmasters over the Hebrew slaves and subjected them to forced labor. Hard service was the name of the game and the Egyptians were ruthless in dealing with the Hebrew slaves (Exod 1:9–14).

This is the stage on which salvation history begins to unfold. And the startling thing is that it begins with the daring action of two Hebrew women slaves, Shiphrah and Puah. They were commanded by Pharaoh, "When you act as midwives to the Hebrew

women, . . . if it is a boy, kill him; but if it is a girl, she shall live"
(Exod 1:16). But the midwives, through a bold and courageous
act of civil disobedience, disobeyed Pharaoh and let the boys live
because they feared God. When Pharaoh questioned them about
their deeds, they explained that the Hebrew women were stronger than the Egyptian women and that they gave birth before the
midwives could arrive at the births. Brueggemann refers to these
women as "carriers of liberation" and contends that "[t]he birth-
ing turns the hopeless into powerful, dangerous hopers."[3] Then
Pharaoh commanded a royal decree that "every boy born to the
Hebrews shall be thrown into the Nile, but every girl shall live"
(Exod 1:22).

Enter Moses, born to a Hebrew woman who saw that she had
given birth to a fine, healthy son. For three months, she hid him,
but when hiding him any longer was impossible, she put her baby
in a papyrus basket, plastered with bitumen and pitch, and placed
it among the reeds on the bank of the river. In due course, Pharaoh's daughter discovered the child, had pity on him, and took
him as her own son.

Consider the implications of what has just happened. Pharaoh
gave a specific command that all male children of the Hebrews be
brutally killed. But not only do Shiphrah and Puah rebel, *Pharaoh's
own daughter rebels!* She specifically goes against her father's command, not only by protecting the baby, but by having the audacity
to bring Moses into her own house, treating him as her own son.

Fast forward. The slaves have been in bondage to Pharaoh
for over four hundred years, and the oppression has become un-
bearable. "The Israelites groaned under their slavery, and . . . their
cry for help rose up to God" (Exod 2:23b). One day, Moses was
tending the flock of his father-in-law Jethro, and God appeared to
Moses in a bush that was burning yet not consumed. "The Lord
said, 'I have observed the misery of my people who are in Egypt;
I have heard their cry on account of their taskmasters. Indeed, I
know their sufferings, and I have come down to deliver them from
the Egyptians, and to bring them up out of that land to a good and

3. Brueggemann, "Exodus," 698.

broad land, a land flowing with milk and honey . . . The cry of the Israelites has now come to me; I have also seen how the Egyptians oppress them. So come, I will send you to Pharaoh to bring my people, the Israelites, out of Egypt'" (Exod 3:7–8a, 9–10). Moses, in essence, says "No way, God!" as he vigorously re-sists the call of God to lead the slaves to freedom. The idea that he should be the one to go to Pharaoh is unthinkable to him, so he offers every excuse he can think of *not* to take part in God's plan. God, however, refuses to take "no" for an answer (see Exod 3:1—4:17 for the exchange between God and Moses). A series of terrifying plagues follows, sent by God upon the Egyptians. God's intention is that each plague will move Pharaoh closer to freeing the slaves, and when the final plague involves the killing of all of Egypt's firstborn, this is the crowning blow, which convinces Pharaoh to rid himself of the entire lot of these trouble-making Hebrew slaves. The Egyptians go so far as to tell them to hurry up, lest something worse befall them.

After they are on their way to freedom, however, Pharaoh reconsiders his position on the slaves. "What was I thinking?" he says to himself in a panic. "The slaves are crucial to the prosper-ity of the empire," and he commands his army, "Go after them! Quickly!" When the freed slaves realize they are being pursued, they also realize that they are trapped. Before them is the sea, and behind them are the chariots and soldiers of Pharaoh. It's as though they are caught between the devil and the deep blue sea. And fear strikes the escaping slaves with a vengeance. "But Moses said to the people, 'Do not be afraid, stand firm, and see the deliverance that the Lord will accomplish for you today; for the Egyptians whom you see today you shall never see again. The Lord will fight for you, and you have only to keep still'" (Exod 14:13–14). Then, as directed by God, Moses stretches out his hand over the sea, and the waters part for the Israelites to cross on dry land and the waters form a wall for them on the right and on the left. But when Moses stretches out his hand over the waters a second time, the sea re-turns to its normal depth, and the Egyptians are drowned. We are told that not one of them is left, and in this act of God, the slaves are saved from the Egyptians.

The soul of this narrative is that God hears the slaves' cries of oppression. But God not only hears, God responds with an outpouring of divine grace toward the downtrodden and, in doing so, God upends the Egyptian empire, creating a new future for those whose lives have been squeezed in the grip of tyranny. We see it first at the end of the second chapter of Exodus when we read that the Israelites "groaned under their slavery" and cried out to God for help. Hearing their cries, God remembers the covenant he made with Abraham, Isaac, and Jacob, and takes notice of their suffering (Exod 2:23b–25). God *remembers*. God *cares* for God's people. God *loves* them. And God is *faithful* to God's covenant.

What does God's faithfulness to God's covenant mean for us today? Are we expected to be faithful to God in response to God's faithfulness to us? Indeed, that is the case. And what does faithfulness to God look like in the American context currently? Does the exodus story give us any clues about what faithfulness looks like in such a world as this? Does it say anything about the civil disobedience that God expects of us at crucial times in our nation's life or about placing our trust in God over against every other claim of authority? Or does it say something about the claims of Jesus that Christians are to live without regard to wealth and superiority over others because that's not what life is all about? What does it mean, after all, to be, first of all, not part of America, but part of the commonwealth of God? In the troubled world in which we are living, these are questions worth pondering.

Pictured in the exodus story is the love of God breaking through the tangled web of terror that human beings inflict on each other and creating a new future for those whose lives were helpless. In other words, *the way things are is not the way things have to be*. Indeed, following the God of the exodus, we are called to explore "countervailing visions about what is *alternatively possible*," and this narrative from our ancient forebears gives us the freedom to reimagine the world in bold new ways. The heart of this story is vibrant hope for those who are beleaguered—a hope that finally cannot be struck down and is lively enough to point to God's new creation even in the direst circumstances. The memory of God's faithfulness in the past, says Walter Brueggemann, enables the Israelite community, and the Christian community, I would add, "to hope against all data and to believe that the *hopelessness* of the data never rules out a different *possibility*. God can indeed work a newness against all the data. God can shatter the known world in order to establish a new historical possibility."[4]

It is impossible to over-emphasize the seminal nature of the exodus story. In Brueggemann's words:

> The "Exodus narrative" itself, the account of the departure of the slave community at the behest of YHWH from the oppression of Pharaoh . . . constitutes the powerful, compelling center of Israel's defining memory of faith, . . . This narrative has become the defining, paradigmatic account of faith whereby Israel is understood as the beloved, chosen community of YHWH and the object of YHWH's peculiar and decisive intervention in public events (see Exod 4:22).[5]

The exodus of the Israelites from slavery in Egypt is indeed the defining event for biblical faith in the Old Testament.

Turning to the Mother of Our Lord for a Sign and a Promise

We see this over and again throughout the Bible, not only in the book of Exodus. What we see in particular is that God rarely if ever settles for the status quo and is always in the process of shaking things up. We see it in the New Testament first in the life of Mary, the mother of Jesus. Mary is visited by the angel Gabriel, who announces that she is going to conceive and bear a son and that she is to name him Jesus. The angel continues, "He will be great, and will be called the Son of the Most High, and the Lord God will give

---

4. Brueggemann, *Hope within History*, 74.

5. Brueggemann, *An Introduction to the Old Testament*, 53.

to him the throne of his ancestor David. He will reign over the house of Jacob forever, and of his kingdom there will be no end." The problem inherent in Gabriel's announcement is that Mary is a virgin, so "How can this be?" she asks. Gabriel explains that the son she is about to bear will come into the world not by natural means, not with the contribution of any masculine prowess, but by the power of the Holy Spirit,[6] and will be called the Son of God (Luke 1:26–28).

Next, Mary goes to visit her relative Elizabeth, who will soon be the mother of John the Baptist, and during her visit there, Mary breaks into song. Among other things, in what we have come to call the *Magnificat*, Mary says that God "has shown strength with his arm [and] has scattered the proud in the thoughts of their hearts. He has brought down the powerful from their thrones, and lifted up the lowly; he has filled the hungry with good things, and sent the rich away empty. He has helped his servant Israel, in remembrance of his mercy, according to the promise he made to our ancestors, to Abraham and to his descendants forever" (Luke 1:51–55).

In other words, Mary is singing about the upside-down world of the God who freed slaves in Egypt, and she is singing about the inside-out world of the gospel that we see in Jesus' challenge to his hometown worshipers in the fourth chapter of Luke (see Introduction). The sign Mary offers us is the upside-down, inside-out world of the living God, and her promise is that we shall be freed from the lesser gods that would consume us. (We'll return to the Magnificat later in the book.)

Cross and Resurrection

We see this upside-down, inside-out world most clearly in the cross and resurrection of Jesus in the New Testament, and specifically we see again that redemption emerges from the miraculous

6. Christopher Morse makes the point that "conceived by the Holy Spirit" indicates "the refusal to believe that male prowess, sexual or otherwise is the source and cause of salvation," in *Not Every Spirit*, 152–53.

intervention of God. Just as the exodus is the defining event in the Old Testament, the cross and resurrection form the defining events in the New Testament. The apostle Paul, in his first letter to the Corinthians, boldly proclaims the good news of salvation: "Now I would remind you, brothers and sisters, of the good news that I proclaimed to you, which you in turn received, in which also you stand . . . For I handed on to you as of first importance what I in turn had received: that Christ died for our sins in accordance with the scriptures, and that he was buried, and that he was raised on the third day in accordance with the scriptures . . ." (1 Cor 15:1, 3–4).

The fact of the matter is that, on a Friday over 2,000 years ago, an angry crowd nailed the Son of God to a cross outside the city of Jerusalem. God's experience with Adam and Eve ends with Adam's and Eve's propensity to sin (Gen 2–3), and the story when we leave it at the end of Genesis 2 is nothing less than tragic. Adam and Eve have eaten of the very tree of which God commanded them not to eat, and in the next chapter, Cain kills Abel in a fit of jealous rage. So now both the divine-human relationship and the relationship between humans are broken. By the time we come to Genesis 6, all creation is so grievous to God that God determines to blot out everything that had once been pronounced "very good" (Gen 1:31). But then God sees in Noah the hope of a new beginning, a fresh start, which leads to the ensuing flood with only those in the ark spared from destruction. Quickly, however, human beings continue to be a huge disappointment to God. By the time we come to Genesis 11, humans have decided that they are so god-like that they build a tower going up into the heavens, seeking to be on par with God. One might say that the human experiment has been a total disaster, and as we read through chapter 11, there is a sense in which a huge question mark is hanging over the entire story. Will God be faithful to God's creation? Or will God return to the previous plan to wipe out all creation?

Enter Abraham and Sarah and the journey to the promised land. The history of Israel begins with this landless, childless couple, following God toward a promised land with the assurance that their progeny will be as numerous as the sands on the seashore. This will be God's fresh beginning, God's new start, and the question mark is no longer hanging over the story. But once the Israelites inherit the promised land, human beings fail to get any better. God gives them a king when they demand it and one king after another leads them to worship the gods of the Canaanites among whom they are living. The kingdom of Israel becomes divided into the northern kingdom of Israel and the southern kingdom of Judah after a squabble between Rehoboam and Jeroboam. The prophets are then sent by God to call the people to repent and turn back to the God who delivered them from slavery in Egypt. God sends the prophets over centuries of time, but by 587 BCE, we find that the Israelites have squandered the entire promised land and no longer have a home there. The northern kingdom of Israel falls to the Assyrians in 722 BCE, and in 587 BCE, the southern kingdom of Judah is taken into exile by the Babylonians. Now what will God do? Once again, a question mark hangs over the entire story, and it hangs there for about 500 years until God decides personally to come to earth in the person of Jesus Christ to show the human race how to live and love. The religious leaders, however, despise him because he refuses to uphold their rules, regulations, and treasured traditions. It's also worth noting that they and their authority are supremely threatened by Jesus' popularity among the people. So, they trump up charges against Jesus, have him condemned to death by the Romans, saying that he claims to be a king, and everyone knows that there is no king except Caesar. Pilate sees right through them, but for political expedience, goes along with the angry mob whom the religious leaders have incited. And they nail him to a cross, the Roman way of executing people, and Jesus dies as a convicted felon. But on the third day, God raises Jesus from the dead and Jesus shows himself to many people. Lest we are tempted, as the church through the ages has unfortunately been, to blame the Jewish community for the crucifixion of Christ, we need to focus our attention on our own repeated betrayal of Christ rather than allow ourselves to die and rise with him.

The apostle Paul affirms the absolute centrality of Jesus Christ when he says: "I decided to know nothing among you except Jesus Christ, and him crucified" (1 Cor 2:2). Paul also speaks often about the direct impact that the crucifixion and resurrection have in the lives of believers. Consider these three passages:

> You were taught to put away your former way of life, your old self, corrupt and deluded by its lusts, and to be renewed in the spirit of your minds, and to clothe yourselves with the new self, created according to the likeness of God in true righteousness and holiness. (Eph 4:22–24)

> We know that our old self was crucified with [Christ] so that the body of sin might be destroyed, and we might no longer be enslaved to sin. For whoever has died is free from sin. But if we have died with Christ, we believe that we will also live with him. (Rom 6:6–8)

> Do not lie to one another, seeing that you have stripped off the old self with its practices and have clothed yourselves with the new self, which is being renewed in knowledge according to the image of its creator. (Col 3:9–10)

What Might This Mean for the Living of Our Lives?

Much has been written about what it means to live the new life in Christ, or to say it another way, to die and rise with Christ. I think the heart of it is *selflessness; being willing to live for the other, even when the other is radically different; being aware that our personal needs and desires are not the only needs and desires that matter in this world; and that we are, as citizens of the commonwealth of God, called to "let justice roll down like waters and righteousness like an ever-flowing stream"* (Amos 5:24).

This has a direct impact on the politics of our day. The clarion cry "America First!" suggests that we as a nation live mainly for ourselves and that the rest of the people in God's creation do not matter as much as we do. Such a view denies that, for disciples of

Jesus Christ, *he is always first* and that we should never attempt to place ourselves at the center of the universe, not to mention the fact that only *some* Americans are allowed to be part of the "America First" slogan. This slogan is in direct opposition to the claims of the gospel.

The inclination to be suspicious of those who are different goes against the grain of "justice rolling down like waters and righteousness like an ever-flowing stream." Jesus one day said to his disciples that if anyone wants to follow him, they need to "take up their cross" and follow him. And what the cross and resurrection show us is that *dying to the old self and rising with Christ* (Rom 6:1–11) is to be the center of our lives, decidedly not proceeding as if we are the center and the rest of world needs to march to be beat of our drum. The Christian life has to do with our willingness to bear witness to Christ's life, death, and resurrection in the lives we lead, to say gladly to our friends and neighbors by the values we hold and the way we live that our old self was "crucified with Christ," and that following Christ means "stripping off the old self with its practices and . . . clothing ourselves with the new self, which is being renewed in knowledge according to the image of its creator" (Col 3:9b–10).

The world as we know it is not the world God wants for the human community, and Christians are called to bear this in mind as political convictions are formed, relationships take shape, and ballots are cast. We are called to ask ourselves not "Which candidate shares my prejudices?" but "Which candidate will bear witness to the good news that God loves all people and will do his or her job with that as a guiding light?" And we are called to participate in the body politic, including the way we vote and the positions we take on various issues, in such a way that *our redemption is the lens through which we view God, neighbor, self, and world.* And redemption means being able to resist the cultural norms that fly in the face of our faith, being able to see the neighbor—even the fundamentally different neighbor—as a brother or sister, and having the freedom to question the world as it is and envision the world in new ways.

We began this chapter with a political act as the servant women Shiphrah and Puah decide that civil disobedience is in order and as Pharaoh finally makes the fateful decision to let the slaves go free. Let's end this chapter with another political act—that of Pontius Pilate. After all, Pilate was, in large measure, trying the keep the political peace when he handed Jesus over to be crucified. He knew in his heart that Jesus had done nothing wrong and did not deserve to die, and that the religious leaders wanted Jesus' head because he had ruffled their feathers one too many times by flaunting unconventional wisdom among leaders with very conventional ideas. Period. End of discussion. But Pilate also saw that he would have a riot on his hands if he failed to hand Jesus over for crucifixion. The crowd was screaming, "Crucify him! Crucify him!" We may think that it was chicken-hearted politics that sent Jesus to the cross, but it was politics that ended up in the salvation of God's creation. We, as ambassadors for Christ, are called to follow the crucified Christ in the values we hold dear, in the positions we take on matters affecting our nation and world, and in the way we vote when we enter the voting booth.

Does this not lead us to love the neighbor who is radically different, honoring the diversity of the human family? Each time we come to the Lord's table in the Sacrament of Holy Communion, we offer a radically subservice act as we foreshadow the scene in Revelation 7:9–17 in which there is "a great multitude that no one could count, from every nation, from all tribes and peoples and languages, standing before the throne" and crying out with a loud voice, "Salvation belongs to our God . . . !" The upshot of this is that the gospel proposes that we live into an alternative reality to the one that appears on the surface of the world, and the new creation God has in mind for the world is such an alternative reality. Are you and I willing to bear witness to God's new creation?

Questions for Discussion—It is assumed that these questions will lead to a conversation that involves exploring the Bible. Please use scripture in giving your answers to the following:

1. Have you ever considered before now that redemption is a political act? Does it make sense the way it is described in this chapter?

2. What are your feelings about civil disobedience? Have you ever participated in it? Do you believe that Shiphrah and Puah did the right thing?

3. Do you identify at all with Moses in his attempt to avoid the call of God? If you are comfortable doing so, name some specifics, in terms of how you have either avoided God's call or answered it in the positive.

4. Does it make sense to you that the exodus is the paradigmatic event in the Old Testament, and the cross and resurrection in the New Testament? Why or why not?

5. What do you think it means to die with Christ and be risen to new life?

6. Do you agree that Pontius Pilate was just trying to please the crowd when he handed Jesus over to be crucified? Why or why not?

4

Politics as Taking Care of God's Good Creation

In this chapter, we come to some of the more controversial issues facing not only us as Americans but the global community as well. In particular, I pose the question, "What is involved in taking care of the creation in which God has placed us, the planet that is our home?"

Humankind Created in the Image of God

My first answer to this question is that taking care of creation means taking care of each other on this planet. To explore this, we need to think about what it means to be created in the image of God, what theologians call the *imago dei*. In Genesis 1:27 we read, "So God created humankind in his image, in the image of God he created them; male and female he created them." What does this mean? It means, first of all, that males and females are equal in God's sight. Neither of the creation stories in Genesis 1 or Genesis 2 reflects a hierarchy of the man dominating the woman. Even in the second creation story, when the woman is created out of the man's rib, it's as if the man says when he sees the woman, "Thank you, God, you finally got it right! This at last is bone of my bones and flesh of my flesh!"

In an essay that he wrote for the journal *Interpretation* back in 2005,[1] W. Sibley Towner begins by recalling a scene from *The Clowns of God*, an excellent novel by Morris West that I read years ago. In the book, the Pope is forced by the Curia to abdicate because he foresaw the apocalypse as an imminent reality. The world is literally falling apart but everyone pretends that it is not. Among other terrible things that are happening, the earth is threatened with nuclear extinction and civil liberties are being violated (does this sound familiar?). Towner writes:

> In the face of all this, the deposed Pope and other dedicated, caring people heroically struggle to save the world from catastrophe, beginning with the most vulnerable, a community of mentally retarded children already marked for extinction in the first round of post-strike triage. These care-givers are convinced that their disabled charges, "God's clowns," are also God's children, that they too bear in their persons the divine image, and that they too deserve the same respect and security demanded by the rich, powerful, mentally able members of the community.[2]

One of the questions we face as a society is whether or not the most vulnerable among us bear the image of God as do the ablest among us and the extent to which we are willing to see all human beings in that light. Towner asks, "Can it be that all of us alike—the saints, the sinners, the able, the differently abled, Christians, jihadists, atheists . . ." display the image of God "to those who have eyes to see?"[3] Do you believe this? Namely, that "every peasant, pauper, and person possesses the gift of God's image"?[4]

Do Muslims possess the image of God as much as Christians do? In many parts of our nation, this is indeed a radical notion,

1. Towner, "Clones of God."
2. Ibid., 341.
3. Ibid., 341.
4. Ibid., 342.

placing the persons who answer "yes" to this question totally outside the limits of acceptability because they are so terribly wrongheaded. It is, however, one of the major claims of the Bible right from the very beginning. *"Adam"* in Hebrew literally means *humankind*. That is to say that Adam and Eve are representative of all human beings. The text is very clear that all human beings have been created in God's image, which calls into question—does it not?—many of our attitudes toward people in the world today. Think what a difference it would make for human relationships if Christian people everywhere were convinced that "every peasant, pauper, and person possesses the gift of God's image"!

That is one issue. Another is the question of what it means to fill and subdue the earth, and to do so bearing God's image in the world. The first chapter of Genesis tells us that God says to the first male and female that they are to "fill the earth and subdue it; and have dominion over the fish of the sea and over the birds of the air and over every living thing that moves upon the earth" (Gen 1:28). In today's world, it means to some people that we have been given carte blanche to do whatever we want with the world's resources. In other words, we are free to exploit creation, to overuse the resources at our disposal and even to deplete them if doing so suits our needs. If you think you need it or want it, then go for it! After all, whatever we want, we deserve to have. Isn't that right? And never mind the "have-nots" of the world. This exposes questions like world hunger, global warming, and whether or not we will one day be held accountable for the way we have taken care of the creation that is God's great gift to the human family. Please notice that I said *the human family*, not only Americans.

"Filling the earth, subduing it, and having dominion over every living thing," of course, raises the issue of stewardship. What does it mean to be faithful stewards of God's good creation? And what does life look like when people are willing to share their wealth with others? It's worth noting that these verses in Genesis 1 occur before what is commonly referred to as the Fall in Genesis 3. In other words, we were called to be faithful stewards *before* we were sinners. In an innocent state, human beings were called to take care of creation. To be faithful stewards of the earth is our first and primary calling, which includes, of course, taking care of each other.

One of the things that I remember reading years ago in the excellent book by A. B. Rhodes, *The Mighty Acts of God*, is that humankind is the "under-sovereign of the Sovereign God."[5] In other words, we are to take care of creation *as God would take care of creation*. That certainly puts a different spin on the issue of stewardship, different that is, from the way the earth's resources are commonly talked about and abused these days.

Rhodes goes on to spell out what he sees as the implications of being created in the image of God. First, humans have a relationship with God that other creatures do not have. Humans may have a unique communion with God and each other—a communion specifically intended for them as human beings. We were created for community. God did not create Adam in isolation. God also created Eve, and Rhodes says that "therefore we must stand in relationship with other human beings as well as with God." Second, Rhodes says that being created in the image of God means that "humankind is the representative of God" on earth. Think for a moment about what that means. The human family is given the high calling right from the beginning to be a mirror of God on the earth. And third, Rhodes suggests that "humankind has a *responsibility* to God. . . . Humankind's superiority to the animals and the responsibility as the under-sovereign of the sovereign God are set forth clearly . . ." in Genesis 1.[6]

My point is that *human beings are not God*. We are called to mirror God's care of the earth, but we are not God. We are *creatures* of God and as creatures we have been given the high calling of living as God wants us to live, not as we would choose to live given the devices and desires of our own hearts, and as Towner says it, our "primacy is no cause for arrogance."[7] Towner goes on to say:

5. Rhodes, *Mighty Acts of God*, 23.

6. Ibid., 23.

7 Towner, "Clones of God," 354.

We are not gods, we are not god-like, we are not even
good much of the time. The full context of the canon of
scripture contains plenty of warnings about our capacity
to make the moral choice of evil, even to the extreme of
crucifying our own Lord. It assures us of our need for
repentance and renewal of our three-fold relationship
with God, each other, and the world. Yet Genesis tells
us that we have a high, God-given vocation, to exercise
dominion in the earth the way God would do it.[8]

The good news is that "the Bible story begins in Gen 1 and not in
Gen 3."[9]

Practical Implications

This raises a whole host of questions about the way the human
family treats the creation that God has given us for our home, the
first of which is global warming. It is popular in some political
circles these days to say that global warming is not happening, and
more pejoratively, that it is an outright hoax. Yet the best scientists
all over the world agree as they refute this claim and contend that
we humans are responsible for the warming temperatures that
are occurring everywhere. And Americans are among the worst
offenders.

Think of our overdependence on oil and the fossil fuel we
emit into the atmosphere on an hourly basis. Fossil fuel is no
friend of the environment in which we live and global warming is
one of the results of it.

The glaciers are melting at the North Pole, putting entire spe-
cies of animals at risk for survival, not to mention the flooding
that will take place elsewhere in the world as the melted ice raises
the sea level. Closer to home, I was interested recently in an article
in *National Geographic* by Daniel Glick in which he talks about
Sperry Glacier in Glacier National Park, Montana, and how the

8. Ibid., 355.
9. Ibid., 354.

U.S. Geological Survey Global Change Research Program is measuring how the park's storied glaciers are melting. Glick writes:

> So far, the results have been positively chilling. When President Taft created Glacier National Park in 1910, it was home to an estimated 150 glaciers. Since then the number has decreased to fewer than 30, and most of those remaining have shrunk in area by two-thirds. [The prediction is] that within 30 years most if not all of the park's namesake glaciers will disappear . . . Scientists who assess the planet's health see indisputable evidence that *Earth has been getting warmer*, in some cases rapidly. Most believe that human activity, in particular the burning of fossil fuels and the resulting buildup of greenhouse gases in the atmosphere, have influenced this warming trend.[10]

Global warming *is* happening and denying it only says that we can live however we want and there will be no consequences. I find it notable that, in another *National Geographic* article, the author says that the issue of whether or not global warming is really happening has generated quite a bit of political controversy in recent years. The article goes on to say that "[a]s scientific knowledge has grown, this debate is moving away from *whether* humans are causing warming and toward questions of *how best to respond*."[11] Again, perhaps the question is, "What if this is more complicated than I have allowed myself to see?"

Elizabeth Hinson-Hasty has written:

> U.S. Senators recently voted to allow drilling in the Arctic National Wildlife Refuge . . . Record oil prices, escalating gas prices, and Americans' fear of losing our hold on the comfortable and convenient life to which we are accustomed was enough to convince the majority of the senate . . . to reduce our dependence on foreign oil. The Senate's conclusion: ensuring American access to fossil fuels is worth plundering one of the last pristine wilderness areas that remain in our nation . . . Is the

10. Glick, "Big Thaw."

11. "Is Global Warming Real?" (emphasis added).

Arctic National Wildlife Refuge to be viewed as a hedge against dependence on foreign oil, or as a sacred trust of incalculable wonder?[12]

The Genesis story does not give human beings, even American human beings, carte blanche to "have dominion" in any way that we see fit, but to do so *as God would have dominion.*

One cannot miss the exclamations of joy in Genesis 1 after each part of creation is formed. "God saw that it was good" is what we read again and again, and finally, God pronounced creation "very good." And these exclamations of joy occur even before human beings are on the scene, suggesting that God has a relationship with the natural world that is positive, an affirmation that human beings are to continue because we were created in God's image.

To go back to A. B. Rhodes, we are only the "under-sovereign of the Sovereign God." This is *God's* creation, not our own. God has entrusted it into our care and will hold us accountable for our stewardship of the earth's resources.

Our comfort and convenience are not primary. *God* is primary and being faithful to God is what the Christian life is all about. Psalm 8, which is reminiscent of Genesis 1, asserts with absolute certainty that this is God's world. Twice in those short nine verses, we read, "O Lord, our Sovereign, how majestic is your name in all the earth!" (Ps 8:1, 9). Psalm 8 also speaks of human dignity, but it both begins and ends with an exclamation that *God's name is majestic in all the earth.* It is nothing less than God's majesty that is at stake in the way we relate to creation. Elizabeth Hinson-Hasty says it this way, "The primary actors in Ps 8 are not human beings, the primary actor is God."[13] And Rosemary Radford Reuther, in her book *Gaia and God,* says that "The biblical witness is one of keen awareness of the limits of human power."[14] We humans take a very dim view of the limits of human power. In many parts of our nation, we think that there are no limits at all.

12. Hinson-Hasty, "Psalm 8," 392.

13. Ibid., 393.

14. Quoted in ibid., 393.

There are of course many other examples of the human plundering and exploitation of creation. Not taking care of the animal world is one, such as killing endangered animals just so we can have the trophy of some animal body part or be able to wear a fur coat in winter. And there are things like strip-mining, deforestation, pollution of the air, rivers, and oceans, and overfishing to the point of depleting part of the world's resources that are nothing less than God's gift to the human family. What would it mean if Christians were to start asking themselves, "How can we live more simply, demanding less of creation?" Maybe then we would mirror God on the earth.

The abuse of God's creation stands in stark contrast to the fact that we have been given a high calling as human beings, namely, to take care of God's world *as God would take care of the world*. As Towner has said it, "We are God's creatures and chosen partners in the work of creation. We are given ever greater opportunity to be bearers of the divine image, that is, positive, responsible stewards in the world, until the day that God makes all things new."[15]

Why Would Anyone Embrace This Way of Life?

In a world culture where those who live among the privileged want what they want when they want it, one of the questions that comes to mind is, "Why would anyone embrace this alternative way of life?" We do so because we are called to take care of creation as God would care for creation *for the sake of each other*. We Americans would do so because we understand that we are but one part of the human family on this planet, and we take care of God's world because we want to reflect God's love for every part of humanity.

Where are you personally with regard to these issues? Do you believe that we Americans plunder and abuse more than we conserve and protect the planet that is our home?

15. Towner, "Clones of God," 356.

Questions for Discussion—It is assumed that these questions will lead to a conversation that involves exploring the Bible. Please use scripture in giving your answers to the following:

1. Do you agree with Sibley Towner that "every peasant, pauper, and person possesses the gift of God's image"? Explain your answer.

2. What does living as the under-sovereign of the Sovereign God look like in the world today?

3. What are your personal beliefs about global warming? Is it a reality or a hoax? Explain your answer.

4. What is your answer to the last question posed in this chapter? Do you believe that we Americans plunder and abuse more than we conserve and protect the planet that is our home? Why or why not?

5

Politics as Taking Care
of Each Other

A Brief Look at Genesis 2

Genesis 2 is chiefly about God's search for a being who is complementary to Adam. In Genesis 2:18, we read that "The Lord God said, 'It is not good that the man should be alone; I will make him a helper as his partner.'" First, God formed every animal of the field and every bird of the air and brought them to the man to see what he would name them, and whatever the man named them, that was its name. But among all the created creatures, we find that "there was not found a helper as his partner" (Gen 2:20c). So God caused a deep sleep to come upon the man and while the man slept, God took one of the man's ribs and made it into a woman. The man then exclaims, "'This at last is bone of my bones and flesh of my flesh; this one shall be called Woman, for out of Man this one was taken'" (Gen 2:23). As I said previously, it's almost as if the man says, "Thank you, God, this is it! This is the creature who will be my partner in life!" And then we read the familiar words, "Therefore a man leaves his father and his mother and clings to his wife, and they become one flesh. And the man and his wife were both naked, and were not ashamed" (Gen 3:24).

Human beings were created for community, for *each other*, and life is to a large degree about exploring and finding ourselves at home in the community of people God has established for us—not only our community as Americans but also the global community of which we are a part. I know that, in some circles, the global community is highly suspect these days. "Beware of the global community!" is the warning we often hear. "Beware of how other countries have historically taken advantage of the United States and how they continue to do so!" These are often the cries of anger and despair that we hear from people who think they are being abused at the hands of the global community. But once again, we are not the primary actors; *God* is the primary actor, and God has placed us in a community that is as broad as all creation. Until we accept this good news and realize that it is, in fact, *good news*, we shall ignore the high calling God has given us in Jesus Christ. We are to love and care for one another in the global community because we are God's people, claimed for this vision of life by Jesus Christ.

The Trinity as a Model for the Kind of Community We Can Become

The Trinity is an exemplary model for the kind of community into which we are called. God is Father, Son, and Holy Spirit—three persons but at the same time One, undivided. What the Father does, the Son and Holy Spirit do; what the Son does, the Father and Holy Spirit do; and what the Holy Spirit does, the Father and the Son do. Think of the reciprocity in this give and take. What is good for one person of the Trinity is good for all three persons of the Trinity. They act together in concert. One person of the Trinity never does what is good for that person alone. What one does is done for all three persons of the Trinity.

Think how different the world would be if we adopted that attitude toward others on the planet. What would happen to our stewardship, for example, if that in which we engage were done for everyone? Imagine the powerful display of love for the neighbor that would represent.

Picture, for a moment, the ancient Israelites in exile in Babylon. They had been brought into exile by the Babylonians who had wrecked the Temple in Jerusalem, torn down the city wall so that it was in shambles, and burned out the palace. Talk about the "other," the Israelites were facing an entire community of the "other." But what does God do? God tells the exiles to pray for the inhabitants of Babylon. "But seek the welfare of the city where I have sent you into exile, and pray to the Lord on its behalf, for in its welfare you will find your welfare" (Jer 29:7). And in securing the welfare of the "other," the future is bright with promise, as God continues to say through Jeremiah: "For surely I know the plans I have for you, says the Lord, plans for your welfare and not for harm, to give you a future with hope" (Jer 29:11). Returning to the Trinity, what would happen if we were to use the model of the Trinity as the lens through which we see various conflicts in the world today? I suggest that it would change the entire landscape of the human family.

Who Is My Neighbor Anyway?

Is the gay person really my neighbor? The straight person? How about the Palestinians—are they my neighbors? Or the Israelis or the Syrians or the Iranians? Or how about the Mexicans? And the list could go on endlessly. Allow me to take us to a passage that asks this question directly, the Parable of the Good Samaritan in Luke 10:25–37. It's a familiar story for many people, but my hunch is that we often miss the deeper meaning. The context is important. Jesus has just finished a prayer in which he thanked God for revealing the things of God's realm to the unlearned rather than to the wise and intelligent, the lowly instead of the high and mighty. In other words, if you consider yourself in the high and mighty realm, you'll probably miss the point. Jesus then turns to a parable that describes in stark and stunning detail the true neighbor. He does so, however, when challenged by a lawyer who asks him,

"Teacher, [testing Jesus] what must I do to inherit eternal life?" Jesus then asks him what he reads in the law, to which the lawyer responds, "You shall love the Lord your God with all your heart, and with all your soul, and with all your strength, and with all your mind; and your neighbor as yourself." Jesus commends the lawyer for giving the right answer. But the lawyer isn't finished with the discussion because we are told that he wanted to justify himself. Seth E. Weeldreyer suggests that the lawyer "seems more concerned about *securing* his own life than *serving* a neighbor."[1] So the lawyer asks point blank, "'And who is my neighbor?' Jesus replied, 'A man was going down from Jerusalem to Jericho, and fell into the hands of robbers, who stripped him, beat him, and went away, leaving him half dead. Both a priest and a Levite came along and passed by on the other side of the dying man. But a Samaritan while traveling came near him; and when he saw him, he was moved with pity.'"

Do you remember the Samaritans? After the fall of the northern kingdom of Israel in 722 BCE, all those who were deemed to have the wherewithal to mount an army and come after the Assyrians were carted off to exile in Assyria. That is to say (without trying to sound too pejorative) that the only people they left behind in Israel were the dregs of the earth. And those they left behind intermarried with others around them, so they were considered half-breeds, not full-fledged Jews, and these were the Samaritans. They certainly were not considered to be Israelites, and by New Testament times, the Jews looked down on them as nobodies, the scum of the earth.

Now while the text doesn't say explicitly that the man who got robbed and beaten was a Jew, I personally think that is fair assumption. The man was stripped, beaten, and left for dead. Not long afterwards, a priest (aka a "religious person" who knew the commandments that the lawyer just identified) saw the man who had been stripped and beaten and was about to die, and he suddenly changed course and passed by on the other side. Similarly, a Levite, who also knew the law, passed by on the other side. Who

1. Weeldreyer, "Luke 10:25–37," 166.

knows? Maybe they were on their way to an important meeting at the synagogue and they were about to be late! Or maybe they didn't know how to help the man and wanted to pretend he wasn't there. Or maybe they were simply afraid. But then a Samaritan comes along and crosses the forbidden boundary *because he is moved with pity*. He ministers to the man's needs, bandaging his wounds, taking him to an inn, and taking care of him. The next day when the Samaritan leaves, he gives the innkeeper some money and says, "Take care of him until I get back, and when I return, I'll reimburse you whatever more you have spent on the man." According to Weeldreyer, this is like "a credit card without limit."[2] In other words, the Samaritan takes care of both the person's present needs and his future needs. Jesus then asks the lawyer which of the three men was a real neighbor to the man who fell into the hands of robbers. The lawyer said, "'The one who showed him mercy.' Jesus said to him, 'Go and do likewise.'"

One way to approach this parable is to ask questions such as, "Where do you find yourself in the parable?" or "With which character do you most identify?" While some of us might identify with the priest or the Levite, others might identify with the Good Samaritan. I doubt, however, that many of us would identify with the one who fell into the hands of robbers. *But what if that is who we are?* And what if one of the reasons Jesus told this parable was so that we would learn to see ourselves as the one who fell into the hands of robbers? Indeed, it takes deep humility for us to identify ourselves as the one who fell into the hands of robbers.

As with other texts in the New Testament, the Parable of the Good Samaritan should not be read as a condemnation of first century priests or Levites. Rather, the text challenges *us*. The crossing of time-honored boundaries is a difficult topic to discuss because it is so rarely done in today's world. It simply is not the way the world turns, is it? We are much more comfortable staying away from the untouchables, the "aliens," or the strangers—those whom our society assures us are misfits and maybe a bit scummy. But this parable shows us the love of God in action. The love of God *does*

2. Ibid., 168.

lead people to cross time-honored boundaries. It *does* lead us to go against the grain of our culture by lifting up the fallen. It *does* move us to pity for those who are wounded and hurting and have no place to lay their heads. Take the Syrian civil war as one example. I learned recently through a Google search that it was reported in April of 2018 that, in the first three and one-half months of 2018, the United States had received only eleven Syrian refugees, who were fleeing the violence of war. "In 2016, near the end of Barack Obama's presidency, the U.S. resettled 15,479 Syrian refugees, according to State Department figures. In 2017, the country let in 3,024. So far this year, that number is just 11. By comparison, over the same 3 1/2-month period in 2016, the U.S. accepted 790."[3] Is this the way to treat our neighbors? Or do we really believe that the Syrians are our neighbors? They are someone's neighbors, but surely not our neighbors as Americans.

These are people who are mired in the most complex and brutal civil war imaginable. They have had chemical weapons used against them by their own president. Their children, their friends, and their neighbors have been killed, and their historic buildings have been demolished. If they ever recover, it will be a long time coming. They have been stripped, beaten, and left for dead. Yet we Americans are acting like the priest and the Levite by passing by on the other side. I don't know about you, but I've got important and timely meetings at the church to which I need to get! I can't concern myself with the Syrians on the other side of the world. Or perhaps letting too many strangers into the United States feels a little scary. And yet the gospel announces the good news that *they are our neighbors.* The same could be said for so many parts of the global community. When was the last time, for example, that you took to heart the plight of the Palestinians and the cruelty done to them by the Israelis and others? I know that the Palestinians have blood on their hands, too, but we should count them as our neighbors as well as the Israelis.

---

3. Amos, "U.S. Has Accepted Only 11."

The good news of the gospel is that all human beings on this earth are our neighbors. Not just people who are like us and share our values and belief system. Not only people who live in a democracy. But *all people*. I'll grant you that many people do not want to act like neighbors and that is a given. At the time of this writing, there is a crisis at the American border with Mexico as the government prohibits people from immigrating to the United States. Government officials are arresting refugees who are fleeing violence and danger instead of helping them as a loving, caring neighbor. Children are taken from their parents at the American border without thought being given to how they will be reunited. Yet God has given the body of the living Christ the love that reminds us that grace is at the center of the Christian life. We read in the Parable of the Good Samaritan, "And who is my neighbor? . . . The one who showed mercy . . . Go and do likewise." We may not be able to open our borders and let everyone who wishes to enter without being vetted and with no plans in place for where and how they will live. But as Christians should we really support policies that treat our neighbors who are victims of war and poverty and violence as our enemies and as threats to our national security?

On the Road to Eternity

The Parable of the Good Samaritan begins with a question about eternity: "Teacher, what must I do to inherit eternal life?" We are reminded that the choices we make here and now are to reflect the eternal life with God toward which we are journeying. Referring to the Parable of the Good Samaritan, Weeldreyer asks this penetrating question: "*Could this text lament lost hospitality in faith relations?*"[4] He then continues:

> Lest we become too assured or pretentious about our faithfulness, remember that Luke's listeners likely esteemed the priest and Levite, expecting a third paradigmatically good passer-by to be a faithful Jew like them.

4. Weeldreyer, "Luke 10:25–37," 168.

Instead it is a Samaritan—stranger, foreigner, person of another faith—through whom we glimpse God's eternal life . . . In biblical texts, mountains, and other high places . . . often serve as the settings for divine activity and communication. Luke reminds us that in Jesus we find God in low places . . . or at least in our willingness to go there.[5]

I hope you see why I said that I fear we often miss the deeper meaning of this parable. Are we willing, for example, to see God reflected in people of different backgrounds than ours, people who look and think differently, people of other faiths?

Feed My Sheep; Take Care of My World

I believe there is a direct link between Genesis 2 and John 21. We've already established that Genesis 2 is about God's creating human beings to be in relationship with each other. In other words, we were created not to live in isolation, but with and for one another. Jesus, in John 21:15–19, places a new twist on this concept by broadening it to include many people. The disciples had fished all night and caught nothing. But after a miraculous haul of fish made possible by the risen Christ, the disciples and Jesus had a huge fish fry there on the beach of a lake. After breakfast, Jesus approached Peter and asked him, "'Simon son of John, do you love me more than these?'" Peter responded by saying, "'Yes, Lord; you know that I love you.' Jesus said to him, 'Feed my lambs.'" Jesus then posed the same question a second time, "'Simon son of John, do you love me?' He said to him, 'Yes, Lord; you know that I love you.' Jesus said to him, 'Tend my sheep.'" But Jesus won't let it rest, asking Peter a third time (mirroring the three times that Peter denied Jesus in the courtyard when Jesus was being interrogated by the authorities?), "'Simon son of John, do you love me?'" By now Peter's feelings are hurt because Jesus won't let up. Finally, Peter says to Jesus, "'Lord, you know everything; you know that I love you.' Jesus said to him, 'Feed my sheep.'" Then we read, "'Very

5. Ibid., 168–69.

truly, I tell you, when you were younger, you used to fasten your own belt and to go wherever you wished. But when you grow old, you will stretch out your hands, and someone else will fasten a belt around you and take you where you do not wish to go.' (He said this to indicate the kind of death by which he would glorify God.) After this he said to him, 'Follow me.'"

This text takes us straight to the heart of the Christian faith, namely, that our faith in Jesus Christ leads us to do outlandish things for people, and yes, even people who are different from us. When Jesus says to Peter, "Feed my lambs . . . tend my sheep . . . feed my sheep," he is in essence saying, "Take care of my people in this world for *they* are my lambs, my sheep, and I want them to be cared for fully." Then, finally, Jesus concludes this scene with a saying about how Peter will die. It will be an event that is painful because it will involve a journey on which Peter does not want to go, and after this radical claim of Jesus, he says to his friend, "Follow me." We don't know for certain, of course, but church tradition says that Peter was crucified upside down.

What I want to emphasize is that there is a cost associated with discipleship. We are not all called to die as Peter did, and not all forms of suffering occur because we are faithful disciples (for example, victims of domestic abuse should not be told to endure their suffering patiently as part of God's calling), but there are concrete ramifications in answering the call to "Follow me," ramifications that will inevitably take us outside our comfort zone and make unexpected demands of us.

This, of course, calls to mind what Jesus says in Mark 8:34b–37: "'If any want to become my followers, let them deny themselves and take up their cross and follow me. For those who want to save their life will lose it, and those who lose their life for my sake, and for the sake of the gospel, will save it. For what will it profit them to gain the whole world and forfeit their life? Indeed, what can they give in return for their life?'"

Following the crucified and risen Lord can be the most difficult proposition in the world. It takes us to places that we never dreamed of going and to people whose lives we never in our wildest imaginations thought we would touch. But taking care of each other is central to the gospel of grace because grace is brimful of love for all the people of God's creation. But where is this grace, I ask you, in the politics of our nation and world as parents and children are separated from each other at the Mexican border and as these children cry for their mothers and fathers? Who is our neighbor? I am baffled by our sympathy for the boys' soccer team in Thailand, who were trapped underground for days on end in 2018, and all the while many people are indifferent to the suffering of the children jailed in our own country. What, after all, are we willing to risk to bind up the wounds of our neighbors who have been abandoned on the side of the road? I am reminded of a hymn that has fallen out of vogue these days, "They Cast Their Nets in Galilee," the final verse of which says: "The peace of God, it is no peace, but strife closed in the sod. Yet, brothers [and sisters] pray but for one thing—the marvelous peace of God."[6]

While following Jesus Christ can indeed be difficult, it is also the most joyous experience one can imagine—joyous even beyond one's imagination. It is joyous because of the grace given in and through the gospel. The peace of God may be no peace, says the hymn, but we are to pray for the marvelous peace of God. God's peace may be difficult on many days, but we do know that it is marvelous!

Do Christians believe this in today's world? And are we willing to act on it?

Questions for Discussion—It is assumed that these questions will lead to a conversation that involves exploring the Bible. Please use scripture in giving your answers to the following:

1. Can you personally see the Trinity as a model for how God wants the human community to live?

2. Do you believe that people living on another continent are our neighbors as Americans? Why or why not?

---

6. William Alexander Percy, "They Cast Their Nets in Galilee" (1924).

3. What are your feelings about the drastic reduction of Syrian refugees our nation is admitting currently? Explain your answer.

4. In the Parable of the Good Samaritan, with which character do you most closely identify? Why?

5. What do think it means to take up our cross and follow Jesus?

6

Overcoming the Temptation to Keep the Gospel Small and Manageable

Through all of my years as a pastor, one of the things I've noticed most often is the desire of both pastors and laypersons to keep the gospel small and manageable, if not to domesticate the gospel altogether. Earlier in this book, I spoke of the desire on the part of many Christians for a less scandalous faith than what the gospel asks of us. The concern of this chapter goes right along with that train of thought.

Years ago, I remember an exercise that I led during a congregation's envisioning the future of its life as a church. I was still young and a little green behind the ears, and I was expecting comments along the lines of social justice and reaching out to the poor in our community. But I'll never forget that one person said that his hope for the future of the church was that a light bulb would be changed in an outside stairwell leading down to the basement of the building!

That is an extreme example of what I'm talking about, but you know what I mean, don't you? It's easier to manage committees and budgets, to plan or listen to sermons, and to get oneself to Sunday school on time than it is it reach out to people who are wounded and broken and hurting beyond belief. But in this chapter, I invite you to think of the gospel of Jesus Christ as immensely larger than life, in fact, as large as all creation. The Bible begins with Genesis 1, a story about the very cosmos itself being called into existence by God, essentially being created out of nothing. Then it ends with the book of Revelation painting a vivid picture of God's new heaven and new earth. No, the gospel is not primarily concerned with whether or not light bulbs get changed and whether or not you and I run our committees professionally and manage our budgets judiciously, although these things, in their own way, are significant. The gospel is about how we are to live faithfully in the creation in which God has placed us with the full realization that we usually do so in the midst of massive turmoil, chaos, and strife.

Do you remember how Genesis 12 begins? It begins with God's promise to Abraham that "in you all the families of the earth shall be blessed." Remember that there is a huge question mark hanging over the human race at the end of the Tower of Babel story in Genesis 11. Things had not worked out with Adam and Eve or Cain and Abel. By the time we get to Genesis 6, God is ready to wash God's hands of the entire human affair, and therefore, the great Flood comes from God as a way of starting creation over with Noah, his wife, and their progeny. But in Genesis 11, we see human beings trying to set themselves on par with God as they build the Tower of Babel. Now what will happen? Will God or won't God remain faithful to the creation that was pronounced "very good." Then in the twelfth chapter, we come to the call of Abraham and we see that he and his wife Sarah will be God's instruments to reclaim a lost creation: "*in you all the families of the earth shall be blessed.*"

Now if we turn to the first chapter of Ephesians in the New Testament, we find Paul saying, "With all wisdom and insight [God] has made known to us the mystery of his will, according to his good pleasure that he set forth in Christ, as a plan for the fullness of time, *to gather up all things in him, things in heaven and things on earth*" (Eph 1:8b–10, emphasis added). I believe that there is a direct link between the concerns of Genesis 12 and

Ephesians 1. Paul is saying that no one and nothing will be left behind, that all people will be gathered up in Jesus Christ, that is, in the cosmic scope of God's love for all creation. And because of that, in the end, God's love will prevail and the human race in all of our diversity will be part of it.

Two Parables of Jesus

As I have suggested, this is a primary theme of the gospel, but at least two parables of Jesus bring this message into sharp relief: the Parable of the Weeds among the Wheat and the Parable of the Fish in the Net, both of which are in Matthew 13. The Parable of the Weeds among the Wheat (Matt 13:24–30) features a person who sowed good seed in his field, but while he slept, an enemy came and sowed weeds among the wheat. When the plants began to sprout, everyone noticed that, not only was there good wheat growing, but weeds also were springing up. The servants of the householder asked him, "If you only planted good seed in the field, then why are there also weeds growing among the wheat. But we know how to handle this," say the servants. "We'll just go out into the field and pull up the weeds so the wheat can grow unfettered." But the householder replies, "'No; for in gathering the weeds you would uproot the wheat along with them. Let both of them grow together until the harvest; and at harvest time I will tell the reapers, Collect the weeds first and bind them in bundles to be burned, but gather the wheat into my barn'" (Matt 13:29–30).

You and I live in a world (and church!) where people like to decide on their own who is good and who is bad, who is "in" and who is "out," those whose lives are good enough for God's realm and those whose lives are not. And not only do we like to do so, we take it upon ourselves to make these decisions and act in this way, as though we ourselves are the final arbiter of right and wrong, good and bad. But the gospel says, "Wait! This world is *God's* field; *God* is the final arbiter; and *God* will make the decisions we often take into our own hands." This parable of Jesus, like the others, represents what it is like in the realm of God. It's not really about a fictitious field, but what it is like to live in God's world and to recognize that the human race really belongs to God, not us. It makes us uncomfortable, but God says to each of us, "Wait a minute! Hold on! Don't be so judgmental!"

Now let's turn to the Parable of the Fish in the Net. It's short and to the point: "Again, the kingdom of heaven is like a net that was thrown into the sea and caught fish of every kind; when it was full, they drew it ashore, sat down, and put the good into baskets but threw out the bad. So it will be at the end of the age. The angels will come out and separate the evil from the righteous and throw them into the furnace of fire, where there will be weeping and gnashing of teeth" (Matt 13:47–50). If you are anything like me, you probably shy away from the language of "furnace of fire" and "weeping and gnashing of teeth." But even if that is the case, care should be taken to note that the *angels* are the ones deciding, based on God's judgment, which of the fish are worth keeping and which ones are not. The point is that *we don't know enough to take the judgment of God into our own hands.* That is not a job that has been given to us.

The point I hope you'll consider is that there is great diversity in the net, just like there is great diversity in the human race. And no doubt the angels will include people who I think are totally unwise to keep. I guarantee you that the angels will make different decisions than you and I would make because the angels will be using the judgment of God.

All of which serves as a stark reminder that we are called to love the neighbor as the self—to love and not to judge. This is so difficult in the world in which we live. There are plenty of neighbors who are hard to love, people we don't want or intend to love. But we live in a diverse world, and in this diversity, everyone is our neighbor. Jesus said that the first and great commandment is to love God with all that is in us—all the heart, soul, mind, and strength. But the second commandment is like the first, namely, to love the neighbor as the self. He didn't say that we are to love only the neighbors with whom we agree and who are like us. Jesus left it broad: "Love the neighbor as the self."

Is There Really an American Exceptionalism?

Sometimes American Christians give in to the temptation to reduce the gospel to size of the United States of America; that is, we think that we are better and more important and worthier of God's grace than the rest of the world. Whenever this happens, I believe it is a misstep that we need to recognize and avoid. I am not saying that we should all aspire to be unpatriotic Americans, but I am saying that there is a difference between patriotism and nationalism. Ryan Hamm has said it this way:

> [I]t's important to make a distinction between patriotism and nationalism . . . Patriotism can be defined simply as love of country . . . Nationalism, on the other hand, takes that love of country and expands it to mean love of country *at the expense of* other nations. It's when someone believes they are better because they come from a particular place, or that someone else is less valuable because of the country that issued their passport. In the United States, it's often given the innocuous sounding title "American exceptionalism . . ." It's saying, "My country is better than yours, and you are less civilized/enlightened/good because of where you are from . . ." [N]ationalism never considers what one's nation could learn from others . . . [T]he Christian's primary allegiance is to God and to [God's] church—which sometimes means the Christian patriot must disagree with her country and do things which might be counterintuitive to "civic duty."[1]

This probably sounds counterintuitive, because this is not the way we usually think, and it certainly is not something we hear many politicians saying today. In a nation of "America First!" it simply makes no sense. But Hamm continues by saying, "Christian neighborliness stretches far beyond national borders and ethnic, political or even religious distinctions. The Church in the United States can joyfully love and serve Mexicans and Syrians, Muslims and atheists, immigrants and refugees because all people, created in the image of God, are our neighbors . . . [Paul] specifically opposed

---

1. Hamm, "Patriotism and Christianity."

nationalism when he called Jewish Christians to recognize their oneness with Gentiles and to stop thinking of themselves as superior."[2]

In the gospel of Jesus Christ, there is no American exceptionalism. It certainly is true that some of America's values and traditions are genuinely exceptional. This country has contributed to the rest of the world in ways that are laudable, and I acknowledge this with deep gratitude. But in the end, in God's realm and in the gospel of Jesus Christ, there is no exceptionalism for any one nation, even the United States.

We would do well to consider the term "nation" in the Bible. There are notable Old Testament texts that are very exclusionary in the sense of saying that God is for Israel alone, and that the Israelites were to keep themselves separate. They were not, for example, to intermarry because that would lead to the worship of other gods. But interestingly in the New Testament, the word "nation" is given a broad meaning indeed because the grace of God is lavishly given in Jesus Christ for all the people of the world. Richard Brand has said, "A nation was being a part of the community of believers, and not a specific piece of land. The Kingdom of God was a kingdom of faith and not political identity. The devotion to one piece of land, one political party, or one particular race of people has very little support in the New Testament.[3] Brand goes on to discuss Psalm 24:1, which says, "The earth is the Lord's and all that is in it, the world, and those who live in it . . ." And based on the psalmist's claim, Brand draws the conclusion that "no nation has or deserves any special privileges or rewards. All land is sacred land. All people in all nations are God's people and God's creation."[4]

Let us return, though, to the Old Testament. One clear illustration of this point is in the book of the prophet Jonah, who doesn't want anything to do with the wretched Ninevites because they are wantonly off the chart when it comes to evil. Jack L. Lundbom reminds us that "Jonah was a nationalistic prophet

2. Ibid.

3. Brand, "Nationalism Is Unchristian."

4. Ibid.

supporting the expansionistic Jeroboam II (2 Kgs 14:25) . . ." Then in the course of the book of Jonah, God holds Jonah's nationalism up to ridicule, Jonah's harsh judgment on a foreign nation causes the utmost repentance, and the Ninevites' repentance causes God to show mercy to the nation of Nineveh,[5] whereupon Jonah goes into a huge funk. (Isn't this the height of divine comedy?) That is the very reason, Jonah says to God, "I fled to Tarshish at the beginning; for I knew that you are a gracious God and merciful, slow to anger, and abounding in steadfast love, and ready to relent from punishing" (Jonah 4:2b). And that is a refrain that we hear often in the Old Testament, not only in Jonah, but also in Exodus, Numbers, Nehemiah, Psalms, and Joel.

All of which brings us back to the grace of God at the center of the Christian life. No person or nation has the privilege of saying "I am God's favorite because he loves me/us better than everyone else!" Remember the Parable of the Laborers in the Vineyard that we discussed in the Introduction? God is generous, and God gives abundantly of divine grace. As the familiar hymn, Amazing Grace, says it, "'Twas grace that taught my heart to fear, and grace my fears relieved."[6] We do well to remember this in the politics of our nation and world. The gospel of Jesus Christ is so much larger than we often imagine it to be. It can never be boiled down to the concerns or the privileges of a single nation, even one's own. As Richard Brand reminds us:

> God doesn't favor one country or one ethnicity over others. Neither should we. "America First" is a perilous policy because it is rooted in self and selfish egoism. It is built on the premise that our needs are more important than your needs, that we're right to value our own lives more than yours . . . Ban Muslims. Build a wall. Penalize businesses that move overseas. Duck out of trade deals. Back away from our commitments to alliances and international organizations. There is nothing neighborly or humble in such policies. The logic of protectionist

5. Lundbom, "Prophets in the Hebrew Bible."
6. John Newton, "Amazing Grace" (1779).

nationalism might lift them up as ultimate goods, but the Gospel tells a different story.[7]

Let us commit ourselves to the gospel's different story and may we do so in a way that honors the broad diversity of the human race.

Reflections on Diversity in the Realm of God

Seeing diversity as a positive thing is hard for many of us, yet the gospel makes this point amazingly clear. One of the clearest examples in the Bible is in Revelation 7:9–17 to which I have already referred. Here we are given a portrait of the new heaven and new earth replete with all the diversity of the human race. In part, here is what we read there: "After this I looked, and there was a great multitude that no one could count, from every nation, from all tribes and peoples and languages, standing before the throne and before the Lamb, robed in white, with palm branches in their hands. They cried out in a loud voice, saying, 'Salvation belongs to our God who is seated on the throne, and to the Lamb!'" (Rev 7:9–10). Then the vision moves to everyone in heaven falling on their faces and worshiping God, singing, "'Amen! Blessing and glory and wisdom and thanksgiving and honor and power and might be to our God forever and ever! Amen'" (Rev 7:12).

This is a vision of a great uncountable multitude made up of people "from every nation, from all tribes and peoples and languages" (Rev 7:9b) worshiping the God of the universe together. There is no distinction, just one huge group of people from all over God's good earth singing praise to the God of their salvation. There is nothing to suggest an "America First!" attitude. There is no "me first" at all. The focus is on *God* and what *God* has done in rescuing the human race from self-destruction. What began as a glorious cosmos in Genesis 1 now comes to a rich conclusion with the human race singing God's praise with a united voice.

This scene of praise carries with it an enormous promise: "They will hunger no more, and thirst no more; the sun will not

---

7. Brand, "Nationalism Is Unchristian."

strike them, nor any scorching heat; for the Lamb at the center of the throne will be their shepherd, and he will guide them to springs of the water of life, and God will wipe away every tear from their eyes" (Rev 7:16–17). Not only will there be a scene of endless praise sung to God, but there will be no more human suffering, no more evil, no more shadows. This is the promise of the gospel!

My question is, "*What if*... what if we were to allow this kind of thinking to enter the politics of our nation and world?" In other words, what would happen if diversity were indeed seen as a positive and not a negative. What would happen if we were to sit down with people with whom we vehemently disagree and try to work out our differences? What would happen should we see people across the world not as a threat but as neighbors? And what would happen if American Christians were to see the entire human race as people for whom Christ died on the cross and rose from the grave? What would happen in this world should people who are rich in material possessions share generously with the poor and began to see the poor as a neighbor rather than a drag on society to be avoided at all costs? What would happen if we should all stop looking out for ourselves as Number One and began to look out for the neighbor as an equal?

The *Book of Order* of the denomination in which I am a minister once said that the church of Jesus Christ is called to be "the provisional demonstration of what God intends for all humanity."[8] On the one hand, that claim sounds a bit audacious, doesn't it? But on the other hand, it is a claim that says we are to witness to God's realm in a world that doesn't yet know it belongs to God. The church is called to model for the world what it means to belong to God first and foremost in this life. Are we willing to take up this calling, no matter what it costs us? Are we willing to see Muslims as neighbors instead of adversaries, and refugees seeking asylum in our nation as neighbors rather than a threat to our national well-being? And are we willing to see leaders of other nations, our allies in particular, not as obstacles to manipulate or ignore or criticize, but as friends with whom we are going sit down together and share

8. *Book of Order*, G-3.0200.

a meal? This—may I suggest?—is what the gospel is all about. And the gospel is indeed as large as all creation.

Questions for Discussion—It is assumed that these questions will lead to a conversation that involves exploring the Bible. Please use scripture in giving your answers to the following:

1. Can you identify ways in which you have noticed in yourself and others the tendency to keep the gospel small and manageable? If so, why do think it is that we do that?

2. What do you make of the distinction in this chapter between patriotism and nationalism?

3. Do you agree with the perspective presented in this chapter that there is no American exceptionalism?

4. In your personal experience, have you had difficulty seeing diversity as a positive? Why or why not?

5. What do make of the scene in Revelation 7 in which many diverse people from all over the world are singing God's praise? Explain your answer.

7

Politics as Social Justice

We now come to a topic that is controversial in the current politics of the United States, namely, social justice. I looked up the term "social justice" in the online *Merriam-Webster Dictionary* and found that it is defined as "a state or doctrine of egalitarianism," which, in turn, is defined as "a belief in human equality especially with respect to social, political, and economic affairs" or a "social philosophy advocating the removal of inequalities among people." In the current political milieu of our nation, I know that I just hit all kinds of political nerves, because the very idea that I am equal to a refugee on the border or a homeless woman is downright offensive. Let's view the term "social justice," however, in the context of the Bible, and to do so, Micah 6 is a good place to begin: *doing justice, loving kindness, and walking humbly with our God* (Mic 6:8b). But what does this mean in a world of closed borders, so-called illegal aliens, refugees seeking sanctuary in our nation, and a shrinking middle class? What does it mean to love *everyone* amid these realities and to be a harbor of welcome for all?

Return with me to Mary's *Magnificat* in Luke 1:46–55 for a moment. There Mary is singing God's praise because God has magnified her soul so that her spirit rejoices in God her Savior.

"[God] has scattered the proud in the thoughts of their hearts. He has brought down the powerful from their thrones, and lifted up the lowly; he has filled the hungry with good things, and sent the rich away empty" (Luke 1:51b–53). There we find a significant clue to the meaning of social justice in the New Testament. The world is literally turned upside down as the lowly are lifted up and the high and mighty ones are brought low. And this is the good news of the gospel.

In the Old Testament, social justice had much to do with taking care of the poor and destitute. We read repeatedly that the Israelites are to care for the widow and the orphan, as well as the resident alien, which is shorthand for the lowest of the low. The term "widow" was more nuanced than it is in our culture. Some scholars argue that it meant more than a woman's husband had died, but that her father-in-law was dead as well, and that she had no adult son to help provide for her economically. Thus, she was in a very vulnerable and lowly position.[1] The term "orphan" is the translation of a Hebrew word, the root of which means "to be alone" or "deprived." In the ancient Near East, all the cultural norms pointed to the male head-of-household as caretaker for everyone in the family. But the orphan was denied this care and was similarly in a vulnerable position.[2] Leviticus tells us that at harvest time, the Israelites were not to reap to the very edges of their fields or gather the gleanings of their harvest. They were instead to leave them for the poor and for the alien (see Lev 19:10 and 23:22). Then we learn that even the resident alien is to be treated with love. We read in Leviticus 19:34 that "[t]he alien who resides with you shall be to you as the citizen among you; you shall love the alien as yourself, for you were aliens in the land of Egypt: I am the Lord your God." This word is deeply troubling in a nation that is hellbent on closing its borders and keeping outsiders away. The alien is to be treated *as the citizen among you*? Really? And we are *to love the alien as ourselves*? You've got to be kidding! Why would we do so?

---

1. Freedman et al., eds., *Eerdmans Dictionary of the Bible*, s.v. "widow."
2. Ibid., s.v. "orphan."

Because we, too, were aliens once and because the Lord is our God and has commanded it.

The Old Testament Prophets

Maybe we prefer a gospel that is less demanding and scandalous. But Lee Griffith says that, if we are looking for moderation, we should never go to the Old Testament prophets. Then Griffith reminds us:

> Abraham Heschel wrote that the prophets are wild and maladjusted. They are maladjusted to the routine suffering that society takes for granted. They are maladjusted to indifference and to the little acts of bloodshed that others regard as regrettable but necessary. The prophets are unreasonable fanatics who pronounce doom on an entire nation because a few widows have been driven from their homes.
>
> In Isaiah, complacency is assailed by the anger of God. Of all people, the chosen people should know that this is a God of justice . . . but the people are not just. This is a God of righteousness . . . but the people are not righteous. This is a God of mercy, compassion and steadfast love . . . but the people are not compassionate. It is a harsh indictment . . . which God is taking into the courtroom of the heavenly council: "Come now, let us argue it out, says the Lord" (Isa 1:18).[3]

While Heschel knew that the Old Testament prophets are wild and maladjusted, he also knew of their deep love not only for God, but *for the people* to whom they prophesy. They shared God's anguish that the people lived as they did, worshiping other gods and abandoning their faith in the God of compassion and mercy for the widow, orphan, and resident alien. But we undoubtedly hear, perhaps because of that love, that the prophets understand how unwavering God is in the demand that God's people stand up for social justice and reach out to touch the lives of the poor and

---

3. Griffith, *God Is Subversive*, 3–5.

needy. And make no mistake, Isaiah is speaking directly to people of faith when he says, "Ah, you who make iniquitous decrees, who write oppressive statutes, to turn aside the needy from justice and to rob the poor of my people of their right, that widows may be your spoil, and that you may make the orphans your prey!" (Isa 10:1–2). Isaiah was not speaking to the godless but to people of faith who had taken up the mantle of godlessness.

Another Old Testament text in this regard is Jeremiah 22:15–16, where a right relationship with God is a matter of social justice. Jeremiah is talking to the son of Josiah who was once a king in the southern kingdom of Judah, and brought about much religious reform. But it was too little, too late, and Josiah's son has definitely not followed in his father's footsteps. Jeremiah gets right up in his face and says, "Did not your father eat and drink and do justice and righteousness? Then it was well with him. He judged the cause of the poor and needy; then it was well. Is not this to know me? says the Lord. But your eyes and heart are only on your dishonest gain, for shedding innocent blood, and for practicing oppression and violence." Let there be no doubt, says Jeremiah: The shedding of innocent blood, the quest for dishonest gain, and the practice of oppression and violence are all opposed to God's will, all of which means that there is much in the politics of our nation and world that is antithetical to the ways of God.

Now let's look together at the prophet Amos whose prophecy was to Israelites "that trample on the needy, and bring to ruin the poor of the land . . ." (Amos 8:4). In other words, he was speaking to those who had lost sight of the fact that doing social justice was central to a right relationship with God. It's helpful to know that Amos did not consider himself first and foremost to be a prophet. He describes himself as "a herdsman, and a dresser of sycamore trees," to whom the Lord said, "Go, prophesy to my people Israel" (Amos 7:14–15). His hometown was Tekoa in the southern kingdom of Judah, but he appears to have been active in the northern cities of Bethel and Samaria.

Picture the scene in your mind's eye. Amos goes to market in the big city and he notices that the wealthy are there and that they are buying the costliest things one can imagine. Every bit of it is unimaginably expensive, but money is no object to the people who are buying like hotcakes the wares that are available. But when he leaves the market, he can't help but notice that all around the market are slums with human need beyond his comprehension. It's a scene in which people don't have two nickels to rub together. As a person of faith and having received the call of God to prophesy, he says to the wealthy who worship God, they think, faithfully: "I hate, I despise your festivals, and I take no delight in your solemn assemblies. Even though you offer me your burnt offerings and grain offerings, I will not accept them; and the offerings of well-being of your fatted animals I will not look upon. Take away from me the noise of your songs; I will not listen to the melody of your harps. But let justice roll down like waters, and righteousness like an ever-flowing stream" (Amos 5:21–24). Through this text, I hear God saying to the churchgoers of our day: *Take away from me the noise of your songs in the sanctuary when you worship on Sunday because I will not countenance your hypocrisy any longer; I have a belly full of it! And stop bringing your offerings because they mean nothing. Make your hearts right by taking care of, not exploiting the poor and downtrodden, and then come and worship me. To truly worship me is to "let justice roll down like waters, and righteousness like an ever-flowing stream"!*

Now it is not a case that God is saying to Christians today, "Shape up or ship out!" I hope it goes without saying that, when disciples of Jesus gather for the worship of God, we do so, in large measure, because we have been forgiven for our failure to do the very thing that the prophet Amos is asking of us. So reading this text christologically, we know that it has become part of the gospel of Jesus Christ to and for us. It goes right along with Mary's *Magnificat* and with the text we considered in the Introduction about Jesus in his hometown synagogue when he outraged his home congregation by saying that the great prophets Elijah and Elisha reached out to Gentiles. And Amos's words also resonate in the stories about Jesus reaching out to the poor and downtrodden, the way he ate with sinners and others who were cast out in his culture, and the knack he had for ministering to the very people on the margins of society. The gospel certainly does nothing to soften this message from Amos, but underscores it in the name of Jesus Christ.

In a similar vein, Griffith says, "To seek justice is to climb down the social ladder and to stand alongside the people who are being battered and dispossessed by the upward momentum of the Great Society," and what is at stake in our relationship with God is these sisters and brothers at the bottom, because the people at the bottom mean more to God than any religious observance or song or offering.[4] *I submit to you that many worshipers and preachers on Sunday morning have no intention of climbing down the social ladder.* Most of us want to return home to our families and friends and daily challenges, seeking to live faithfully, but not willing to make sacrifices for the strangers who need our attention. And I don't know about you, but I find this extremely convicting, and I find myself wondering about the depth of my own faith, as well as the faith of the church.

I find it helpful that there have been people in the nineteenth and twentieth centuries who have worked strenuously for social justice. People such as Washington Gladden (1836–1918), Walter Rauschenbusch (1861–1918), and Martin Luther King Jr. (1929–1968) all worked tirelessly as they followed in the footsteps of the Old Testament prophets, as well as Jesus himself. In his lifetime, Gladden earned the title as "the father of the American Social Gospel."[5] Rauschenbusch typified the passion of the Social Gospel and its soul. "Nearly every motif of the Social Gospel . . . came to expression in his works . . . He subjected the American social order to informed analysis and found it wanting. He awakened compassion for human suffering and proposed realistic reforms. He delineated the key concept of the 'Kingdom of God on earth' with persuasive clarity. And finally, he overcame apathy and pessimism with a stirring vision of the coming kingdom." He was

4. Ibid., 11.

5. Ahlstrom, *Religious History of the American People*, 791.

often "a lonely prophet."[6] And Martin Luther King Jr. took on the enormous task of the non-violent Civil Rights Movement in the 1950s and 1960s. King's personal involvement began with bus riots in 1955 and ended in 1968 when an assassin's bullet took his life. It is important, in my view, to see the Civil Rights Movement as rooted in King's understanding of the gospel and his relationship with Jesus Christ. Accused by some as a troublemaker, he was really an American prophet, and as the Bible tells us, prophets are not always popular.

Other Biblical Texts to Shape Us

Turn with me now to Luke 16:19–31, which is the Parable of the Rich Man and Lazarus. It tells the story of a rich man who wined and dined with the best, and lived as high on the hog as a person could possibly live. But at his door was a homeless man named Lazarus who was as down-and-out as he could be. Lazarus longed to satisfy his hunger from the crumbs that fell from the rich man's table, and the dogs would come and lick the sores that covered his body. Well, in the passage of time, Lazarus died and so did the rich man. The angels came and carried the poor man to be with Abraham, while the rich man found himself tormented in Hades.[7] The rich man looked up, however, and could see Abraham far off in the distance with Lazarus at his side, whereupon the rich man begged father Abraham for mercy. But father Abraham told the rich man, "'Child, remember that during your lifetime you received your good things, and Lazarus in like manner evil things; but now he is comforted here, and you are in agony. Besides all this, between you and us a great chasm has been fixed, so that those who might want

6. Ibid., 800.

7. According to Jim West in *Eerdmans Dictionary of the Bible*, Hades was "[o]riginally the name of the Greek god of the underworld, but later the name of the underworld itself . . . [and] is translated 'hell' in most English versions of the Bible." In the Septuagint (the Greek version of the Hebrew Bible), however, the word "Hades" is used for Sheol. "Hades became in Hellenistic thought a place of torment. It is this understanding of hell as the torture chamber of eternity which influenced the NT writers."

to pass from here to you cannot do so, and no one can cross from there to us.'" The rich man then pleaded for his five brothers that someone could go and warn them so that they would not come to the same fate. "Abraham replied, 'They have Moses and the prophets; they should listen to them.' He said, 'No, father Abraham; but if someone goes to them from the dead, they will repent.' He said to him, 'If they do not listen to Moses and the prophets, neither will they be convinced even if someone rises from the dead.'"

What does this parable say to a church in which Christ, risen from the dead, is the center? Again, I find myself convicted to the core when I realize who Lazarus is in our midst today. Lazarus is a gay couple for whom a baker has refused to bake a cake for their wedding because of "religious" convictions. Lazarus is the Syrian refugee who has no place to lay her head. He is the child separated from his parents at the border because there is no place for them in this country. And Lazarus is the national leader who has been spurned by the United States because the United States has supposedly been exploited through the years by its allies. And Lazarus is the multitude of people whose lives will be affected by global warming in a nation, many of whose leaders deny that it even exists. Yes, the day is coming when there will a great deal for which we must answer.

One wonders if Charles Dickens had this text in mind when Scrooge's partner returns from the grave to warn him about the price he'll pay for his lack of generosity towards those in need. Scrooge scoffs at him. As the text says, if he wouldn't listen to the prophets, why would he listen to someone who came back from the dead? But Scrooge finally does heed the warnings of the three spirits that visited him on Christmas Eve. Will we?

Do you remember the story of Cain and Abel in Genesis 4:1–16? There Cain murders his brother Abel because he assumes that God favors Abel more than him because God apparently liked Abel's offering more than Cain's. The text says simply that "the Lord had regard for Abel and his offering, but for Cain and his offering he had no regard." It does not say that God doesn't love Cain or that Cain is no longer acceptable to God. But you see, Cain has a problem. He doesn't just want to be loved by God; he wants to be loved better than Abel. And when he doesn't see this working out, he murders his brother one day in cold blood. God asks Cain why his countenance has fallen and why he is angry. "If you do well, will you not be accepted? And if you don't do well, sin is lurking at the door; it desires you," but Cain did not follow the Lord's advice to master the evil that was at the very door of his life. Do you remember Cain's smart-aleck retort to God? After the murder, God asks Cain, "Where is your brother?" and Cain's response is "How should I know? Am I my brother's keeper?" This encapsulates the issue that has plagued the human race ever since Cain murdered his brother Abel: *learning to live peaceably with others.* On any given day, you pick up the daily newspaper or turn to your computer or handheld device for news, and it's clear that we are still dealing with this issue and doing so on an international scale.

Now come with me to Acts 10:1–48, which is a story about Peter, Cornelius, and the inclusion of the Gentiles (which includes me) in the gospel. In Caesarea, there lived a centurion named Cornelius, who was a member of the Italian Cohort, in other words, a Gentile. But Cornelius feared God, gave generously for the benefit of the poor and prayed constantly to God. About three o'clock one afternoon, Cornelius had a vision in which an angel of God said to him, "Your prayers and your alms have ascended as a memorial before God. Now send men to Joppa for a certain Simon who is called Peter . . ." and the angel told Cornelius where Peter could be found in Joppa. Cornelius then sent two servants, as well as a devout solider, to Joppa where they were to find Peter and bring him back. About noon the next day, Peter went up on his roof to pray and became hungry. While his food was being prepared, he fell into a trance in which "[h]e saw the heaven opened and something like a large sheet coming down, being lowered to the ground by its four corners. In it were all kinds of four-footed creatures and reptiles and birds of the air. Then he heard a voice saying, 'Get up, Peter; kill and eat.'" Peter said, "No way, Lord, for I have never eaten anything that is profane or unclean." The voice said to him, "What God has made clean, you must not call profane."

This happened three times, and the thing was suddenly taken up to heaven. While Peter was in a state of puzzlement, the men sent by Cornelius appeared. Peter asked them why they had come, and they responded by saying, "Cornelius, a centurion, an upright and God-fearing man, who is well spoken of by the whole Jewish nation, was directed by a holy angel to send for you to come to his house and to hear what you have to say." So the next morning, Peter got up and went with these three strangers. When they arrived back at Cornelius's house, upon meeting Peter, Cornelius fell at his feet and worshiped him. But Peter insisted that Cornelius get up, saying to him, "'I am only a mortal.' And as he talked with him, he went in and found that many had assembled; and he said to them, 'You yourselves know that it is unlawful for a Jew to associate with or to visit a Gentile; but God has shown me that I should not call anyone profane or unclean. So when I was sent for, I came without objection. Now may I ask why you sent for me?'"

Cornelius then told him about his vision four days earlier and how he had been told, "'Cornelius, your prayer has been heard and your alms have been remembered before God. Send therefore to Joppa and ask for Simon, who is called Peter . . .' Therefore I sent for you immediately, and you have been kind enough to come. So now all of us are here in the presence of God to listen to all that the Lord has commanded you to say."

Then Peter said to them that he has come to understand that "God shows no partiality, but in every nation anyone who fears him and does what is right is acceptable to him." Peter then told the assembled crowd the gospel story, culminating in the death and resurrection of Jesus Christ, and "[w]hile Peter was still speaking, the Holy Spirit fell upon all who had heard the word." The circumcised believers who were present were amazed that the Holy Spirit had been given even to the Gentiles, and Peter called for the Gentiles to be baptized.

The key sentence for me in the rather long story is this: "What God has made clean, you must not call profane." Remember that this story relies on the idea that no responsible, self-respecting Jew would countenance a Gentile. The Gentiles were truly forbidden territory, beyond the pale, and were a despised lot. But God said to Peter that everyone is welcome in God's realm.

Who is in the despised lot in today's world? Each of us could probably come up with a pretty good list. But remember this: "What God has made clean, you must not call profane." And if God can make Gentiles clean, God can make anyone clean. I happen to be living proof of this good news! Paul said to the Galatians (and to us) that the whole law of God can be summed up with this one commandment, "You shall love your neighbor as yourself" (Gal 5:14). He, of course, was quoting none other than our Lord Jesus Christ in the Synoptic Gospels (Matt 22:19; Mark 12:31; Luke 10:27). Am I my neighbor's (brother's) keeper? The answer the story itself gives to this question is: "No, you are not your neighbor's keeper, in the sense of being her or his supervisor, but you are to relate to the "other" in your life as a brother or sister. You are to care for the neighbor like a brother or sister. In that sense, you indeed are your neighbor's keeper."

Who is our neighbor? *Everyone with whom we share this planet, which is not our creation, but God's creation!* Brothers and sisters in Christ, the church of Jesus Christ is called to tear down the walls of race and bigotry that divide so many people all over the globe. That's what it means for the church to be "the provisional demonstration of what God intends for all humanity,"[8] declaring that the reign of God is not only a future promise, but also a present reality. You and I are called to show this present reality in our relationships with the people in our lives. With whom will those relationships be? And as we form those relationships, will we "let justice roll down like waters, and righteousness like an ever-flowing stream"?

Of course, the answer to this question is, "No, probably not." But our failure to do so isn't the end of the story. The good news of the gospel is that, through the gospel, Jesus Christ has already "Let justice roll down like waters, and righteousness like an ever-flowing stream." And because he has already done so, we know that there is hope for us, and that we are forgiven when we fail.

8. *Book of Order*, G-3.0200.

Thanks be to God for the generous hope and forgiveness that are our inheritance in Jesus Christ.

Questions for Discussion—It is assumed that these questions will lead to a conversation that involves exploring the Bible. Please use scripture in giving your answers to the following:

1. Do you believe with Mary the mother of our Lord that God is engaged in scattering the proud in the thoughts of their hearts, bringing down the powerful from their thrones, and lifting up the lowly, and that God is in the process of filling the hungry with good things, and sending the rich away empty? Why or why not? In what way might this be the meaning of Good Friday and Easter?

2. What are your feelings about the passage cited in Leviticus, saying that the resident aliens are to be treated *as citizens among us* and that we are *to love the aliens as ourselves*? Explain your answer.

3. What are your thoughts on climbing down the social ladder to stand with those who have been battered by the storms of life in this world?

4. What do you believe it means to follow the call of God as we hear it through the prophet Amos, to "let justice roll down like waters and righteousness like an ever-flowing stream"? Do you see this happening in your congregation? If it is, how might you further that ministry? And if it is not, how might you be a change agent to begin something new?

5. When it comes right down to it, do you believe that everyone on this planet is our neighbor?

8

Overcoming the Fear Factor

What drives much of what goes on in our world today is fear of the "other." Dietrich Bonhoeffer once wrote of the spiritual damage that fear causes: "It crouches in people's hearts," he wrote, and it "hollows out their insides . . . and secretly gnaws and eats away at all the ties that bind a person to God and to others."[1] This is a season of fear in the United States as well as in the global community. We fear another terrorist attack. We fear another shooting or a person driving a car on a sidewalk that will kill people. We fear people who are different from us, like Muslins, for example. We fear people who are gay or transgender. Democrats sometimes fear Republicans and vice versa. Israelis fear Palestinians and Palestinians fear Israelis. And I could continue this list of fears a *ad infinitum*. The point is that we live in a world in which people fear one another, and I am sure you have noticed that we get a daily dose of fear from our politicians in Washington, D.C. As Peter W. Marty, the publisher of *The Christian Century*, said in a recent editorial, "It's not an overstatement to say there's a fear epidemic in America these days. Swapping stories of fright has become our national pastime. It has always been true that if you want to kill

1. Marty, "From the Publisher," 3. The original quotation can be found in Bonhoeffer, "Overcoming Fear, Matthew 8:23–27," 60.

an idea, a piece of legislation, or another person's dignity, you just get people good and scared of what that idea, policy, or person might do."[2] We would do well to remember that in the Bible, God's response to human fear is, "Trust me for I will keep you; I will keep your life." The psalmist assures us in no uncertain terms that "[t]he Lord will keep your going out and your coming in from this time on and forevermore" (Ps 121:8). That's why Marty goes on to say that "[t]hose of us who don't want our insides hollowed out, or the biblical and moral ties that bind us to God and one another severed, lean on a savior."[3]

I wholeheartedly affirm what Marty has said. We *do* lean on a savior. But I would be so bold as to suggest that we also have one another in the church on whom to lean. In Chapter 1, I said that the church is called to be a laboratory for seeing life, including our politics, through the lens of the gospel as we help one another along life's journey. Now as I bring this book to a close, I want to dig in on this very point.

In the same issue of *The Christian Century* from which the Marty quotes were taken, there is an article by Amy Frykholm who talks about various settings in which people along different parts of the political divide in our nation sit down together and share a meal, after which they tell their personal stories of both pain and compromise. One of the groups called "the People's Supper" provides a conversation guide and some basic principles for the conversation that will follow supper. "Typical discussion starters for an initial bridging supper are "How and when did you first learn about being a citizen?" "Talk about a time when you felt excluded, threatened, or unwelcome." "Talk about a time when you felt welcome and safe." "Talk about a spiritual practice that is giving you strength at this time." "What stories from your tradition inspire you to be your most courageous self?"[4]

It is significant to note that our Lord often practiced table hospitality with people. He sat down at table with his disciples,

2. Ibid, 3.

3. Ibid, 3.

4. Frykholm, "Around a Table," 10.

as they were his closest friends, but also repeatedly with sinners and other outcasts, much to the dismay and disapproval of the religious leaders. He did so because sitting down to share a meal is and intimate and hospitable thing to do. So there is good precedent for the People's Supper.

While there is good precedent for it, it also represents an inherent risk, but if what Micky Scottbey Jones calls a "brave space"[5] is created, such a supper can lead to a conversation in which people are open and honest about themselves and how they relate to others along the political divide. My sense, however, is that we fear difference too much in today's church for this to happen with any kind of consistency or regularity, so we end up talking about politics with those we know are on our "side," people who we know in advance are going to agree with us.

Typically, however, the settings discussed in this article were those in which a dinner was announced, people registered in advance, and then found themselves talking to complete strangers about things that are deeply personal. If that can happen among strangers, why doesn't it happen in the church of Jesus Christ? The book of Ephesians says that "speaking the truth in love," is part of growing up "in every way into him who is the head, into Christ . . ." (Eph 4:15). This occurs in a section about unity within the body of Christ, and the affirmation could not be more clear that *speaking the truth in love to each other is part of what it means to be a disciple of Jesus Christ.* So not only do we have a savior on whom to lean, we have each other on whom to lean.

Frykholm says that the settings she describes offered opportunities for people "to ask people questions and to listen carefully," and that "people told stories about painful divisions in their churches, or about their upbringings and what they had learned of politics from their parents."[6] There is a group Frykholm describes called "Better Angels" that seeks to bring conservatives and liberals together in an intensely moderated event. She said that the family therapist who leads the group says that "The Reds tend to

5. Ibid., 10.
6. Ibid., 11.

feel shamed by the Blues to a much greater extent than the Blues realize, and are often reluctant to enter into a conversation with Blues for fear of further shaming. Often the reason the Reds attend such events is because they offer a chance to 'de-monsterize' themselves."[7]

I personally believe that we often fail to realize that we are all wounded people, and that we all feel like we have been "monsterized" or demonized to some degree by the other "side." If that is indeed the case, then one of our highest callings is to hold up each other in the church, to see one another as wounded people who are in the church because we all need to experience the love of God given so lavishly in Jesus Christ *through each other*. The church needs to provide more occasions for people to converse with each other and to listen carefully to those whose views are different from their own. We need to be able to hear a person say that she or he feels demonized and why. And disciples of Jesus need a brave space for this to happen. The church of Jesus Christ is called to be that kind of brave space.

One woman involved in the People's Supper says that "I am feeling challenged in this season to revisit the first two chapters of Genesis: the creation story and the imaging of divine light that God says exists in all of us . . . That means I need to find God present in people that I strongly disagree with . . . If I am going to bear my cross and preach in my actions what it means to embody the radical love ethic of Christ, then I see myself preparing tables for people I love, because they are wounded."[8] I say again: all of us are wounded and we all feel demonized by the other "side." The church is called to be the very context in which our differences can be laid on the table and we can both love and be loved in spite of those differences.

I want to end this book where it began—with the grace of God active and flung widely in the world. Like the one planting the seed flung it indiscriminately, so it is with God's grace. As I said previously, "'Twas grace that taught my heart to fear, and grace my

7. Ibid., 11.

8. Ibid., 12.

fears relieved." Because of God's grace, we need not fear each other, even if we are on the opposite side of the ideological/political spectrum. Grace leads us to be there for one another, and grace enables us to overcome the fear factor in our lives. The grace of God leads us to one another and will, in the end, lead us home to God.

Questions for Discussion—It is assumed that these questions will lead to a conversation that involves exploring the Bible. Please use scripture in giving your answers to the following:

1. Do you agree that God has given us each other on whom to lean for this kind of conversation?

2. Do you personally believe that the church needs to have political discussion? Or does it make you too uncomfortable?

3. Would you feel free to say what you think in such a setting? Why or why not?

Bibliography

Ahlstrom, Sydney E. *A Religious History of the American People*. New Haven, CT: Yale University Press, 1972.

Amos, Deborah. "The U.S. Has Accepted Only 11 Refugees This Year." *All Things Considered*, National Public Radio, April 12, 2018. https://www.npr.org/sections/parallels/2018/04/12/602022877/the-u-s-has-welcomed-only-11-syrian-refugees-this-year.

Amsterdam, Anthony G., and Jerome Bruner. *Minding the Law*. Cambridge, MA: Harvard University Press, 2000.

Bonhoeffer, Dietrich. *Ethics*. Dietrich Bonhoeffer Works 6. Edited by Clifford J. Green, translated by Reinhard Krauss, Charles C. West, and Douglas W. Stott. Minneapolis: Fortress, 2005.

———. *Life Together*. Dietrich Bonhoeffer Works 5. Edited by Geffrey B. Kelly, translated by Daniel W. Bloesch and James H. Burtness. Minneapolis: Fortress, 2005.

———. "Overcoming Fear, Matthew 8:23–27." In *The Collected Sermons of Dietrich Bonhoeffer*, edited by Isabel Best. Minneapolis: Fortress, 2012.

Book of Order. 2009–11 ed. Louisville: Presbyterian Church (U.S.A.) Office of the General Assembly, 2009.

Boring, M. Eugene. "The Gospel of Matthew." In *The New Interpreter's Bible*, vol. 8. Nashville: Abingdon, 1995.

Brand, Richard. "Nationalism Is Unchristian." *Huffington Post*, March 13, 2017. https://huffingtonpost.com/entry/nationalism-is-unchristian_us_58c705ece4b022817b29160d.

"A Brief Statement of Faith—Presbyterian Church (U.S.A.)." In *Book of Confessions: Study Edition*. Louisville: Geneva, Presbyterian Church (U.S.A.) Office of the General Assembly, 1996.

Brueggemann, Walter. "Exodus." In *The New Interpreter's Bible*, vol. 1. Nashville: Abingdon, 1994.

———. *Genesis*. Interpretation. Atlanta: John Knox, 1982.

———. *Hope within History*. Atlanta: John Knox, 1987.

———. *An Introduction to the Old Testament: The Canon and Christian Imagination*. Louisville: Westminster John Knox, 2003.

Bibliography

———. *The Land: Place as Gift, Promise, and Challenge in Biblical Faith.* Overtures to Biblical Theology. Philadelphia: Fortress, 1977.

Buechner, Frederick. *Now and Then.* San Francisco: Harper & Row, 1991.

Capon, Robert Farrar. *The Parables of the Kingdom.* Grand Rapids: Zondervan, 1985.

The Confession of 1967—Inclusive Language Version. Presbyterian Church (U.S.A.) Office of Theology and Worship, 2002.

Copenhaver, Martin B. "It Can Be Dangerous." *Pulpit Digest*, January/February, 1995.

Freedman, Daivd Noel, Allen C. Myers, and Astrid B. Beck, editors. *Eerdmans Dictionary of the Bible.* Grand Rapids: Eerdmans, 2000.

Frykholm, Amy. "Around a Table: The People's Supper Engages Political Difference." *The Christian Century*, July 4, 2018.

Glick, Daniel. "The Big Thaw." *National Geographic.* https://www.national geographic.com/environment/global-warming/big-thaw/.

Griffith, Lee. *God Is Subversive: Talking Peace in a Time of Empire.* Grand Rapids: Eerdmans, 2011.

Hallie, Philip. *Lest Innocent Blood Be Shed.* New York: Harper & Row, 1979.

Hamm, Ryan. "Patriotism and Christianity." *Christian Bible Studies*, June 26, 2012. https://www.christianitytoday.com/biblestudies/articles/churchhome leadership/patriotism.html.

Hinson-Hasty, Elizabeth. "Psalm 8." *Interpretation* 39, no. 4 (October 2005).

"Is Global Warming Real?" *National Geographic.* https://www.nationalgeographic .com/environment/global-warming/global-warming-real/.

Long, Thomas G. *Matthew.* Westminster Bible Companion. Louisville: Westminster John Knox, 1997.

Lundbom, Jack R. "Prophets in the Hebrew Bible." *Oxford Research Encyclopedia of Religion.* May 2016. http://religion.oxfordre.com/view/10.1093/acrefore /9780199340378.001.0001/acrefore-9780199340378-e-109.

Marty, Peter W. "From the Publisher." *The Christian Century*, June 4, 2018.

Morse, Christopher. *Not Every Spirit: A Dogmatics of Christian Disbelief.* Valley Forge, PA: Trinity, 1994.

Peterson, Eugene H. "Eat This Book." *Theology Today* 56, no. 1 (April 1999) 5–17.

Plantinga, Cornelius, Jr. *Not the Way It's Supposed to Be: A Breviary of Sin.* Grand Rapids: Eerdmans, 1995.

Reuther, Rosemary Radford. *Gaia and God: An Ecofeminist Theology of Earth Healing.* New York: HarperCollins, 1992.

Rhodes, Arnold B. *The Mighty Acts of God.* Rev. ed. Revised by W. Eugene March. Louisville: Geneva, 2000.

Towner, W. Sibley. "Clones of God: Genesis 1:26–28 and the Image of God in the Hebrew Bible." *Interpretation* 39, no. 4 (October 2005) 341–56.

Volf, Miroslav. *Exclusion and Embrace: A Theological Exploration of Identity, Otherness, and Reconciliation.* Nashville: Abingdon, 1996.

Bibliography

Weeldreyer, Seth E. "Luke 10:25–37." *Interpretation* 62, no. 2 (April 2008) 166–69.

West, Morris. *The Clowns of God.* New York: Morrow, 1981.

Willimon, William H. *Preaching Master Class: Lessons from Will Willimon's Five-Minute Preaching Workshop.* Edited by Noel A. Snyder. Art for Faith's Sake 4. Eugene, OR: Cascade, 2010.

Yancy, Philip. *Soul Survivor: How Thirteen Unlikely Mentors Helped My Faith Survive the Church.* Colorado Springs: Waterbrook, 2003.

Made in the USA
Monee, IL
06 September 2022